I0559038

Kingdom Psalms

Modern Kingdom Psalm caters to every one- the rich, the poor, the happy, the depressed, the saint and the sinner. These uplifting writings have their own unique style that will provide comfort and direction to any and all readers. This is not just a revised or translated edition of biblical psalms, but is instead a completely new collection of psalms that speak about current events and issues that are happening in today's world, while also sharing the author's inspirational personal testimony.

The time to give praises to Jehovah God is always.

1. Always is the time for praise and the season for thanksgiving; for God's ways are magnanimous and his multitude of blessings numberless.

2. Therefore we aught not to limit the praise we give to him or schedule the time of our thanksgiving for him.

3. Always is the time for praise; so let praise continuously pour out of the mouths from the very depths of our hearts and the illuminated charms of our spirit.

4. No matter how numerous our praises are, they can never compensate for the countless blessings already bestowed on us or those blessings yet to come.

5. The blessings of God flow by the moment and fall by the second; for we cannot live a millisecond without them.

6. Therefore we aught to always be mindful of his goodness and appreciate him with our always praise.

7. For his divine worthiness far surpass our frail ability to applaud and to honor him.

8. Even the very breath that we breathe is a blessing from God and an element of his grace.

9. Therefore we aught to praise God always because always is the time to praise him.

10. Let all the saints say Amen.

Pastor Oswald Skippings

Leavitt Peak Press

ISBN: 978-1-969865-44-2 (sc)
ISBN: 978-1-969865-45-9 (e)

Rev. date: 11/11/2025

KINGDOM PSALMS

Pastor Oswald Skippings

Dedication

I dedicate this book of psalms to all of you readers that sacrifice your valuable time to read and study its contents. It is my desire and sincere hope that not only your spiritual life be enriched, but that you are empowered to walk boldly and confidently in the liberty with which Christ has made you free. It is also my desire that consequently you be drawn to experience a closer daily walk with Jesus the Christ.

CONTENTS

Foreword

Kudos to Former Parliamentarian, Philanthropist, and Biblical Scholar, the Hon. Oswald O'Neil Skippings, Former Chief Minister of the Turks and Caicos Islands, in completing the "long awaited", Kingdom Psalms. This book, which is a compilation of sacred, poetic writings, reflect human suffering, rebellion, divine justice, love, prayer of repentance, and songs of praise to The Almighty God.

The book is written in lyrical prose that evokes an ineffable beauty of God's creation, amidst a turbulent world. Furthermore, each theme categorizes life experiences and emotions that are resolved through meditation, reflection, repentance, and recognition of God, as the Supreme Being.

Extracts from Kingdom Psalms have touched the hearts and soul of many, as well as transformed the lives of those seeking solace, and a clearer understanding of the Holy Scriptures.

It is therefore through this text, that the author encourages Skeptics, Unbelievers, and those who are downtrodden and depressed, to look to the Hills of Zion, from whence cometh their help, and they will surely discover, that their help cometh from the Lord, who made heaven and earth (Psalm 121:1-2).

Finally, these poetic declarations are timely, and relevant to our present-day cares in life. However, as FAITH is an attribute that aligns us with God's heart in overcoming worry and the vicissitudes of life, we are able through FAITH, to declare these Kingdom Psalms, and experience a remarkable change in our lives. Many thanks Brother Skippings, in "heeding the call" to complete this book, via the talent and inspiration, God has given you.

Dr. Portia Brown-Jordan
Renowned Educator, Evangelist, and Author of New York Times Best Seller: Herbal Medicine and Home Remedies: A Potpourri in Bahamian Culture
https://edenstriuneministries.word press.com

Preface

These psalms represent a flood of inspiration that has flowed from the Holy Spirit into my spirit. Indeed they are consistent with the word of God as outlined on the Holy Bible. They delve into the multi facets of Jehovah God. It is explicit to the reader that God is love and longsuffering, while at the same time God is a God of vengeance, and his reprimand could indeed be terrible.

This work also teaches us that Kingdom living is what is expected of the latter day saints. One of its many themes is spiritual romance between God and man, which is experienced through the beauty of praise and the inspiration of worship. For God is love and God is a spirit, and Christ himself tell us, "But the hour cometh and now is, when the true worshippers shall worship the father, in Spirit and in truth; for the father seeketh such to worship him" (John 4:23 KJV).

Because it is extremely important particularly to the babes in Christ, it is explicit throughout these psalms that the Almighty, true and living, creator God is Jehovah and not just any abstract symbol of power chosen by the worshipper or his denominational sect.

There is something in this work for everyone; the rich, the poor, the happy, the depressed, the saint, and the sinner. Everyone can find direction to God, comfort in their time of distress and solace, strength and encouragement in their time of weakness and doubt.

It is therefore my hope that these psalms would be a lamp unto the feet of its readers and a light unto their path. From the penned words, you may find life through he anointing of the Holy Spirit and the source of your daily bread.

Sacrifice of Praise

All glory, praise, honor and exaltation be to the Almighty God Jehovah, whose name is excellent and glorious and is exalted above all blessing and praise. Nevertheless, you have magnified your word above all your name; for your word, oh God, is potent and alive, and gives life and light to all who diligently seek after truth and righteousness.

To Jesus the Messiah and Christ, your only begotten son, who alone is able to save. He is able to save even through his holy name: for it is the only name under heaven, throughout the entire universe whereby men may be saved.

The King of Kings, The Lord of Lords, The Conquering Lion of the Tribe of Judah, the mighty God. Hallelujah! The Prince of Peace, the Alpha and Omega, the Beginning and End, I lift up hallowed praises from unworthy lips, with clean hands that you have cleansed and from a pure heart that you have purged, because of your bountiful grace and tender mercies.

To the Holy Spirit of God, my teacher and reminder, my guide and comforter, my strength and my instructor, you are the holy dimension of God who empowers me, O spirit of holiness and power of the blessed resurrection; I honor you and adore you.

After I was drawn by you, I repented and believed and was redeemed by the precious blood of Jesus Christ; then you sealed me unto the day of redemption. For you are the Holy Spirit of promise whom Christ sent after his glorious departure to heaven, where he sits at the right hand of his father. You are the revealer of divine truths and hidden secrets of the Kingdom of God. So you enlighten the imaginations of the children of God with privileged truths and divine revelations reserved for the elect of God.

You are the truth who testify of Christ because he is truth, and even me you guide into all truths and show me the mystery of things past and things yet to come. It is you, Holy Spirit, who gives me the prophetic word and enlightens me through dreams and visions.

Praise be to you oh blessed Holy Spirit, my most eloquent spokesman, my intrinsic inspiration and motivation. You anoint me with supernatural power and endow me with the utterance of other tongues, even some that are spoken in a heavenly language that confuses the enemy and is beyond his comprehension-even the understanding of Satan.

You are my invincible defender, for I live with the blessed assurance that when my enemy comes upon me, you shall lift up a standard against him, and he has to fall at my feet in defeat as I triumph in victory. So I give you immeasurable thanks and tribute, because you too are God.

Again to the triune God: three in one, three yet one. The God of love, peace, joy and longsuffering; the God of salvation, deliverance and sanctification unto holiness and righteousness; Jehovah God.

You alone are deserving of all the praise, all the glory, all the exaltation, and all the honor; in majestic reverence I magnify your holiness. For you alone are high, lifted up and exalted in majesty and glory; you have created all things in the heavens and in the earth for your pleasure, even man, whom you have exalted above every creature and given dominion over the entire earth.

Yet when man had transgressed and fallen from his glory, you in your infinite wisdom had already through divine preparation designed a way of redemption, salvation and regeneration through the precious blood of Jesus Christ the Lamb of God, to take away the sins of the world. You sent us the Christ, who alone is able to redeem us and give us that perfect peace that passes all human understanding and that agape love that surpasses all human love.

Hallelujah, hallelujah, hallelujah to you oh Jehovah my God! Let the highest praise be my motto and my continuous sacrifice, and let my body be a living, sacrifice, holy and acceptable to you, my gracious God. For you are excellent, flawless and righteous in all your ways. I love you God with all my heart, my mind, my body and my soul.

Now Lord, I bow and kneel in total submission to do your bidding as you desire and direct; all in the mighty name of Jesus Christ, the volunteered sacrificial lamb and Savior of a lost and dying world.

Jehovah is eternal and lives forever and ever. Amen.

PART ONE

Kingdom Psalm 1

I have determined to make your praise and your worship my mindset.

Blessed is my deliverer, your praise lace my lips all day long, as an anthem of the saints that's forever melodious and sweet.

2. There is no joy like the joy of praise and the joy of worship; for when your name is exalted my heart is joyful and my spirit is refreshed.

3. While my praise glorify you O redeemer, it empowers my spirit and saturate my mind with heavenly thoughts; they put me in heavenly places, even on the threshold of heaven itself.

4. I cannot cease to praise you, for therein lies my joy in you; and within my joy in you, lies my strength; and within my strength in you, lies my righteousness; and within my righteousness, lies my endurance.

5. For my salvation is guaranteed at the end of my endurance in this holy race.

6. Even my imaginations praise you, for even my meditation in my daily walk is saturated with your praise.

7. My very fantasies O Lord are a byproduct of the praise that I usher up to you.

8. I have determined to make your praise and your worship my mindset. It is then that fruitfulness abounds, and the fruit of the Spirit mushrooms and blossoms in the lives of your saints.

9. Experience has taught me that praise and worship to you invoke the abundant downpour of your blessings and your anointing.

10. It is then that burdens are lifted, stress is relieved, chains of bondage are broken, and deliverance is forth-coming.

11. Praises open the door of my heart to receive the multiplicity of blessings that you have prepared for me. It gives me a receiving, thankful and appreciative heart.

12. So let my breath be a wind of praise, my voice be a noise of praise, my ears be hearers of praise, and my eyes see visions of praise.

13. May excellence in praise forever more, be yours O Lord and savior God.

Kingdom Psalm 2

Righteousness is my goal and faithfulness is my path to achieve it.

The inspiration of right cousness is far more gratifying than a mine of diamonds.

2. For while diamonds please the eye, righteousness satisfies the soul of the godly, and inspires him to dance in the courts of the Almighty God.

3. Righteousness was ordained of God from the beginning; but the evil one snatched it away from Adam and Eve.

4. For they were not watchful and fruitful in their spirit. In blindness and error they yielded their authority to the evil one.

5. But Jehovah is still merciful in that he sent yet another son; he is the last Adam, his only begotten son.

6. He suffered and died for our transgression and offers us redemption and restoration.

7. Hence I am able to bask in righteousness as a son of God and a son of light.

8. He reestablished my authority and restored the integrity of my righteousness; thus my joy is fulfilled.

9. So I will abide in the safety of his divinity forever and ever. There I am safe from even the wicked one.

10. For his arm of the evil one is powerless against the Almighty God of Zion, and against his sons and daughters who abide under his shadow.

11. Jehovah protects his own and provides safety and impenetrable shelter to his begotten.

12. Jesus, I thank you for sending the Holy Spirit so that you have not left me comfortless nor ignorant.

13. But I have a divine professor who instructs me, for he is a reminder of your word and of your deeds.

14. He is an informer of secrets, a revealer of your intentions, and a giver of your instructions.

15. So righteousness is my goal, and faithfulness is my path to achieve it.

16. I love you O Lord, with the same love that you have bestowed upon me in so much abundance.

17. Even on the cross you have delivered me from all guilt and unrighteousness; let my life be a light to the dark-ness of this world.

18. May I deliver you as a beacon of hope to the hope-less and an inspiration to the despondent.

19. Let me be a doer of your will on earth as it is in heaven; let me be worthy of delivering the proclamation of salvation to the lost and

20. For salvation is brought into the world by Jesus the Christ for all the lost souls.

21. Empower me O Lord to be a sower in your kingdom and to labor selflessly in your harvest.

22. Put a halt to the enlargement of the borders of hell and enlarge your kingdom O God.

23. Have mercy my God, have mercy.

Kingdom Psalm 3

Divinely ordained prosperity

Take pleasure in walking with God, and delight in his ways.

2. There is no greater joy and fulfillment than the joy of relationship and the pleasure of fellowship with the creator.

3. For there is no void in the saint's life, except there is no fellowship with God: and who can fill the void except God.

4. The pursuit of happiness is but a fleeting illusion, except God is being pursued in his righteousness.

5. God alone is fulfillment; that's why the rich man is miserable in the courts of the devil.

6. For his wealth hangs around his neck like an albatross; it brings worry, frustration and misery.

7. But joy and peace come with grace and mercy; their source is not money and material wealth, but their source is Jesus Christ.

8. For wealth is not prosperity, but prosperity is lodged in the bank vaults of salvation and redemption.

9. They are neither coated with silver nor plated with gold, but they are covered with the crimson blood of the lamb that was slain from the foundation of the world. Hallelujah!

10. So delight in the riches of God, for they are free yet priceless and everlasting.

11. They cannot depreciate in value, but their interests are ever accruing, and their rewards eternal and holy.

12. For the interest of material wealth to the ungodly accrue misery, unfulfillment and death.

13. Therefore, only the wise discern the lasting treasures and pursue them with relentless diligence and with a godly heart.

14. Prosperity lies in the richness of righteousness.

15. Amen O Jehovah.

Kingdom Psalm 4

Trust God for all your needs and seek not the gifts of the unrighteous.

Beware of the helping hand of the wicked; for his help often comes with a costly price.

2. Seek not gifts from the corrupt hands of the unjust; his gifs are wrapped with a ribbon of expectation.

3. A day of reconciliation is inevitable when the consequences of his unreasonable demands far outweigh the value of his gifts.

4. His gifts are often designed to extract compromise in return.

5. They seek to impugn the integrity of your office and compromise your righteous standing in Christ.

6. Be aware that all gifts that come from God are good, and the motive is pure.

7. So examine carefully the extended hand of every evil giver; for the greater part of his gift is usually the concealed expectation to receive in return.

8. Walk in wisdom and operate in discernment. For the children of God should circumvent reproach and walk blamelessly in the kingdom of God.

9. We enjoy the divine privilege of being called after the impeccable name of Jehovah God.

10. His holy name is beyond reproach and his righteousness cannot be impugned.

11. Therefore, be comforted in your need by the assurance that your God is able to supply them all.

12. Indeed he is able to supply them from the reserves of his abundant riches in the heavens.

13. Moreover, he is always cognizant of every need that you may have, and he is zealous in his desire to fill them.

14. If you walk in his statutes and first of all pursue the things of the kingdom, then your needs shall be met automatically. That is God's promise to the sons of God.

15. So walk in faith and claim his promises; for he is faithful and committed to every promise he makes.

16. Serve Jehovah in sincerity of heart, for he is a faithful and loving God who is attentive to the needs of his children.

17. Holy is the name of the Lord, and righteous are all his works always and forever. Amen.

Kingdom Psalm 5

Jehovah is a faithful friend to all; but the hand of men is treacherous.

Oh wicked men, open your blinded eyes; turn from your ungodly ways, for they pave a path that leads to death.

2. Forsake the ways of sin and evil; rebuke your companions who lure you into a way of unrighteousness.

3. They are not your friends because they do not love you; but they are hell bent on seeing you destroyed and sentenced to a chaotic pit of aggravation and eternal torment.

4. Choose friends whose desire is that you live the abundant life, and who are desirous of seeing you do good and shun evil.

5. The ways of the wicked are treacherous and destructive, and their reward is calamitous.

6. Seek out the God of salvation, for he is awaiting you. In fact, he has been reaching out his hand to you to help you, to deliver you and to save you.

7. His name is Jehovah, and there is no other God like him. He knows all, he sees all, and he is everywhere all the time.

8. It is he who is the God of love and the giver of grace and mercy to all mankind.

9. It is he who created you for his purpose, to give you joy, prosperity, peace and eternal life

10. He is the one who protects you even now in your daily walk; it is he who stays the cold icy hands of death from snatching you away prematurely.

11. Sing praises unto him; glorify his name and acknowledge him as Lord and savior; he will deliver you from the ways of destruction.

12. He will direct you into the ways of life and the paths of light and righteousness. Give him the chance to deliver you.

13. O wicked man, there is merit in serving Jehovah God and benefits in living in his kingdom.

14. He is a rewarding God and all his rewards for righteousness are good, pleasant and prosperous.

15. Be not fooled and deceived as Eve in the Garden of Eden; for Satan is pursuing hard after your soul to destroy you, but Jehovah is the one who loves you and who can save you from the evil one.

16. Surrender today because there is no better time than now; this is your moment of destiny; this is your admonition; embrace your invitation.

17. Heed the words of wisdom. For I too have trodden that path of destruction. But I have received wise counsel and turned to Jehovah God.

18. He has received me with open arms and enlightened me with wisdom; he has showered me with love, com-passion and understanding.

19. He listens intently and hears my complaints, and is a solver of problems; for even the impossible is made possible by him.

20. O man of the world, listen intently to the words of wisdom, for only a fool follows hard after death.

Kingdom Psalm 6

Jehovah loves even the wicked and relentlessly pursues them with a righteous hand of deliverance.

In ignorance does the heathen despise God; for God is his infinite creator and the keeper of his very soul.

2. God abhors the ignorance of the heathen, but 8. loves his soul and is desirous of salvaging it to inhabit his glorious kingdom for all eternity.

3. His folly does not go unnoticed by the ever-watchful eye of God; nor does his transgression go unrecorded.

4. Even while he delights in mischief and revels in sin, God stays his hand of wrath and offers the olive branch of love and peace to his wretched soul.

5. God waves a banner of love over his head and shines light into the darkness that engulfs him.

6. Even while he refuses the light of life and chooses the darkness of death, God still woos him with divine agape love and offers him eternal life.

7. But the heathen is not aware of the power of the word and the anointing of the Holy Spirit of God; but I can testify that they are potent and powerful.

8. For they stalk him with good and righteous intentions, and they offer him invaluable promises.

9. God persists in his righteous pursuit because he is love. It is his innate desire to save the lost and redeem his darkened heart with the light of his son Jesus Christ.

10. Who else is so long-suffering; who else is so merciful and tolerant; who else is so caring and loving even to his enemies?

11. Therefore, the righteous ought to always praise God with a thankful heart, for he too was once lost in sin and blinded by the darkness of ignorance.

12. Yet the same God Jehovah delivered him in due time; thus he removed his shroud of ignorance.

13. Those who have been delivered ought to learn the ways of God; they ought to be patient, longsuffering and loving to the children of dark-ness. For love fosters under-standing and invokes trust; perfect love transforms even the children of darkness.

14. Let the righteous entreat the wicked with perfect love and enduring patience; let the sons and daughters of God deposit the seed of the word in his heart.

15. It will bear fruit in due season; water it with prayer and supplication to God on behalf of the wicked. For the word will not return to God without bearing fruit.

16. Let's elevate the wicked with prayer; let's con-found him with the word; and let's pursue him with fervent prayer and fasting.

17. For he is God's creation, and it is for him that Christ died on the cross and resurrected again from the dead.

18. It is for him that Christ escaped the clutches of death and defeated the foreboding entrapment of the grave.

19. Now the saints of God must throw out our fishing lines and cast out our nets.

20. For Christ has made us fishers of the heathen, that we may bring them into the kingdom of righteousness.

21. He had designated us fishers of lost men, that we may deliver them from the engulfing sea of destruction and bring them into the ark of safety.

22. May the grace of God continue to reign on the heathen until his heart is pierced, and until it is contrite and he yields to the light of righteousness.

23. O mighty God of the universe, you are relentless in the righteous pursuit of the wicked. Hallelujah!

24. Jehovah, you are just in all your ways and mighty to save the lost from death and destruction.

25. Hallowed be the holy name of Jehovah God.

Kingdom Psalm 7

Exalt God and diligently seek knowledge from him. Spiritual knowledge is spiritual power.

Rejoice O you partakers of the Kingdom of Heaven. Sing, dance and celebrate O children of light, for you are the privileged sons of God.

2. Delight yourselves in praise and hold fast to great expectations, for you are seated in heavenly places in Christ Jesus and are only pilgrims of this decaying earth.

3. Search out the heart of 8. Jehovah; seek out his ways; for the long awaited hour of your enlightenment is here, and there are troves of mysterious treasures and a multitude of precious secrets hidden deep inside his heart.

4. For God had reserved them as precious diamonds and invaluable rubies for this hour; but only his chosen sons who are diligent and studious and who are searchers of his heart will he enlighten.

5. Jehovah alone is the revealer of end time revelations. Do not be content with yesterdays knowledge; neither be satisfied with the wisdom of old.

6. Sons of light beware of complacency and shed the garment of spiritual mediocrity; for it is a killer of dreams and a crusher of visions.

7. As sons you must therefore have a relationship with your father and fellow-ship with your God. There is no substitute for intimacy with father God.

8. For only as trusted, loving sons and daughters will you be entrusted with the priceless nuggets of the kingdom.

9. The father wants his children to be armed with privileged knowledge of the kingdom: for knowledge is power and power establishes authority.

10. So entreat your father and beseech your God; but let your motives be holy and your intentions honorable; let your desire be to glorify God and exalt his mighty name in the entire earth.

11. Let the intents of your heart be pleasing and uplifting to God; and he will delight in you; he will confide in you and expose his thoughts and reveal his intentions.

12. Jehovah will unravel his enigmatic mysteries even to the uneducated, to the widow, the orphan and the prisoner, as long as there is purity and sincerity of heart.

13. Worship Jehovah, exalt his name, magnify his very presence; seek to publish his name and proclaim his fame to all nationalities, especially to those who are the outcast of society.

14. Enter the prison gates with pleasure of heart and entreat those that are incarcerated; offer them true freedom and everlasting peace through Christ Jesus.

15. Let the heathen know that our God is almighty and worthy of praise and exaltation. Testify of his endless grace and unmatchable mercy.

16. Search out his heart and petition him in prayer and supplication.

17. Eat sumptuously of his holy word and feast continuous on it; for therein lie the keys for the revelation of his thoughts.

18. Yet be mindful that Jehovah is God; it is his option to choose whom he wills; even so, to enlighten whoso-ever he desires to fulfill his divine will and purpose.

19. Give Jehovah the glory, for he alone is the most exalted God.

Kingdom Psalm 8

The name of the Lord is mighty and resourceful; he is our source.

Jehovah Jireh, the promises in your names are exceedingly great, but the power to deliver is even greater.

2. Great and many are the expectations of the sons of God; because their father is almighty and his promises easy to deliver.

3. Your name oh God, is the epitome of glory, power and might.

4. In your name are deliverance, healing and provision; indeed, you are the source of every need, every commodity, and every resource.

5. You alone O Lord can boast of absolute complete-ness; you alone can deliver total fulfillment. That is because you alone are our creator and source.

6. Jehovah, you are our replenisher and restorer; our reviver and rejuvenator; and the all-inclusive provider of every need we may have, be it spiritual, emotional or physical.

7. So I take refuge in your names because they are my unyielding, unshakable fortress and my invincible garrison.

8. Just the thought of the power, the glory, and the might of your name make the wicked tremble and faint at your feet. For none can with-stand the onslaught of your awesome and overwhelming power.

9. But I find delight in them all; because I am your son and not an outcast; I am your soldier and not a rebel; I am your saint and not a sinner; I am your friend and not your foe.

10. Therefore my praises to your name are unwavering, for I usher in the morning with salutations of praises to your name, and bid the sunset goodbye with your worship.

11. The safety and comfort in your name is immeasurable; it is more than sufficient, for the saints of God.

12. It is a refuge that is reserved for the righteous but is available to every sinner who repents and diligently pursues righteousness.

13. For you are not partial to nationality, socio-economic status or ethnic background; but only to the sincerity of the heart.

14. You are just and righteous in all your dealings because your name is holy, unimpeachable and beyond reproach.

15. Forever blessed and mighty be the name of Jehovah, the most high God, whose throne sits in the invisible portal's glory. Amen and amen.

Kingdom Psalm 9

The ways of God are unfathomable.

The ways of Jehovah are beyond fathoming; and his thoughts cannot be determined except by revelation of his Holy Spirit.

2. I was exalted high among men and held in high esteem.

3. My prominence was declared by the stroke of the pen of men and the desire of his heart.

4. Jehovah saw fit to intervene and tear down my earthly glory; He demoted me in the kingdom of man and promoted me in the kingdom of heaven. Sholaba!

5. How excellent are your ways oh God, and how astute is your judgment.

6. To be a messenger in the kingdom of God is far more joyous, prominent and rewarding than being a president in the kingdom of men.

7. In the kingdom of God your benefits are eternal; all the promises are true and delivered, and your assurances are guaranteed by divine powers that are un-changeable and supreme.

8. Because you are God, all your judgments are righteous and perfect; because you are God, there are no unsolvable problems and no insurmountable hurdles; but you alone specialize in impossibilities.

9. Your resources are unlimited and do not dwindle.

10. Moreover, you are creator of all the natural resources and all the wealth that is in the entire universe.

11. You are the God of pro-vision, and this is the season of increase.

12. Therefore, your sons and daughters are filthy rich.

13. We know that true prosperity is only experienced by the royal priesthood, the peculiar people, the chosen generation and the holy nation of God.

14. For wealth is not measured by the amount of money in our bank accounts, but by the amount of godliness that is in our hearts.

15. That is why we praise you all day long; because you do dwell in the praises of your saints.

16. We crave after you O God Jehovah; we long for the constant anointing of your Holy Spirit; we abide in your son Jesus Christ and secure a place for his abode in our hearts.

17. Therein lies the richness of the children of the kingdom; therein lies the wealth of the sons and daughters of God; therein lies our promotion, for all promotion is of God.

18. In you O God we are complete and lack nothing whatsoever.

Kingdom Psalm 10

The conclusion of the wicked is damnation.

Holy fire falls on the head of the righteous to anoint and empower them; but on the head of the reprobate, to bring them damnation and destruction.

2. For the wicked toil in the vineyard of sin and demand its due wage; there-fore, they shall not escape death.

3. However, eternal life is the inheritance of the children of righteousness alone, for death cowers in fear and crumbles in defeat at their anointed feet.

4. The wicked is synonymous with death and can only be delivered through Christ's redeeming blood; blood that is more righteous even than that of Abel.

5. For only the Lamb of God has the blood of salvation, deliverance, and redemption; therefore, he alone can transform unrighteousness to righteousness.

6. Destruction stalks the unjust like a deadly shadow; there is no safety for him except the blood of the Lamb of God.

7. That is why I walk in the shadow of the almighty and shower in the blood of Christ; for the blood of Christ is off limits to Satan and his demons.

8. They cannot withstand its anointed power of righteousness.

9. But it is a refuge to the righteous and a disinfectant to the impurities of sin.

10. The unrighteous walk on uncharted highways cluttered with sin and condemnation.

11. The wicked are led by the blind destroyer whose ways are evi and whose end is destruction, misery and devastation.

12. But the highways of the righteous are paved with divine graze and mercy.

13. Because the righteous are led by the Holy Spirit of God, their end is eternal and everlasting joy.

14. The destination of the righteous is being prepared by the Messiah in the holy heavens, by he who sits next to the majestic throne of God.

15. But the conclusion of the unrighteous is in a bottomless pit with the deceiver, the liar and the deadly evil dragon.

16. Therefore, I have made Jehovah my refuge and his kingdom my place of abode.

17. For even the new heaven, the new Jerusalem and the new earth shall be my dwelling place.

PART TWO

Kingdom Psalm 11

The sons of light overpower the sons of darkness, for light takes authority over darkness.

I will arise from the pit of complacency. With a full arsenal of righteous weaponry will I arise, ready for Jihad against the kingdom of darkness.

2. Ready to fight the holy war of Jehovah and smite Satan from every side even as David mote the evil Goliath.

3. The enemy is vulnerable because you are almighty, and you have already defeated him on the cross of Calvary O Christ.

4. It is you that has bruised his head, and dealt him a bitter blow of defeat.

5. We are your saints; we are your revolutionaries, armed and dangerous with the power of righteousness.

6. Therefore we are willing, ready and able to inflict serious damage to the kingdom of darkness and elevate the kingdom of light.

7. Give us the fire O Lord through your Holy Spirit, so that even our words may purge the contrite hearts of the sinner.

8. Let the dreadful flames consume the evil ploy of the enemy; that they shall acknowledge your majestic eminence O Christ.

9. For your throne is exalted and magnified in the heaven of heavens; you sit on the right hand of the father Jehovah with power and might.

10. For even so you were given all power in heaven and in the earth.

11. Your almighty power enables us to move a mountain as a pebble, and to bind a demon and cast him into outer darkness.

12. This is your kingdom and we are your subjects, for we are soldiers in the army of the most high.

13. We are the aggressors and we are leading the attack on the enemy; and put the enemy on the defensive because we fear no evil.

14. We are the superior children of light, and we overshadow the children of darkness.

15. We are over comers because you abide in us and we abide in you.

16. Therefore we are the grater ones with the greater power; because there is no power except what comes from Jehovah.

17. We are the children of light and cannot be defeated; darkness has no power over light.

18. Light is the conqueror over darkness; light is the suppressor of darkness.

19. It eliminates darkness with its glorious presence.

20. Therefore, whenever light appears on the scene, darkness retreats.

21. It takes refuge further into itself and finds comfort and security in its retreat into further darkness.

22. For it dreads the awesome power of light.

23. So as children of light, we declare and decree our daily victory over the prince of darkness and over his sons of perdition.

24. For the victory rests in the hands of the righteous every time.

25. Because we are the children of the holy light.

Kingdom Psalm 12

The fool and the heretic defy and denounce God; they are deceived by their darkened soul.

Who can defy the arm of Jehovah the holy one, the designer, architect and creator of this great universe?

2. The one who is high and lifted up in the heaven of heavens.

3. The one who is exalted above every other god and exceeds and surpasses every power and principality:

4. They scatter before him like straw in a hurricane and are driven from his presence.

5. Who can withstand the fury of a terrible God; or endure the heat of his consuming fire?

6. He alone is righteous in his judgments but fierce in his anger toward the pre-sumptuous transgressor.

7. Also toward those who seek to discredit the power and the honor of his holy name.

8. Therefore, be wise and refrain from tempting the almighty one.

9. Pray even to him for grace and mercy; that he may contain his wrath and withhold his fury.

10. It is a dreadful and nerve wrecking thing to fall into the hands of Jehovah God and be subject to his wrath.

11. Jah is the only one in all the universe who is justified in his vengeful ways.

12. For when the creature provokes the creator to jealousy, he disrespects and rejects his supreme sovereignty and his power.

13. Retribution belongs to the creator; for creation is his, and the kingdom is his.

14. Even the celestial throne is his almighty seat of authority.

15. Therefore, total respect, honor and reverence are our due diligence to him and him alone.

16. Yet in ignorance and arrogance the fool rises in defiance of the power and authority of our creator God.

17. He rages like the heathen and snarl the teeth that the creator has fashioned.

18. He foolishly attempts to bite the hand that provides his daily bread.

19. In disrespect, rude-ness and ungratefulness, he rants and rave.

20. Even our dogs are spared from this dishonorable treatment and are pampered by the hands that God made and praised from the lips that God fashioned.

21. His mercies endure forever. But there is a time and a season for his wrath and his vengeance; for he has already spoken it.

22. For he who defies and denounces the Almighty God has declared himself a fool and a heretic.

23. If his foolish ways continue in arrogance, he is courting sudden destruction; death is his guaranteed lot.

24. For Jehovah is not to be tempted, nor is his counsel to be rejected in arrogance.

25. Even his longsuffering comes to a bitter end for the defiant and arrogant transgressor.

26. May the guilty and foolish exercise wisdom and tempt not Jehovah anymore.

27. Rather may he repent from his evil ways; then he will pardon him from the well of his mercy.

28. Take heed to warning all you transgressors who revel in vanity and take plea-sure in disobedience.

29. Turn to God with a repentant heart; for he will be merciful and pardon you.

30. Then will he shower you from the river of his grace.

31. Oh magnify Jah on his glorious throne, for he is everlasting and eternal.

Kingdom Psalm 13

My protection is divine and Impenetrable.

Because my redeemer is alive, I am not afraid of the wiles of the devil or the threats of my enemies.

2. Their threats are not threatening to me; nor is their intimidation in the least intimidating.

3. At night I sleep in serene peace and relaxing comfort, resting in the ever-lasting arms of the conquering Lion of the tribe of Judah.

4. Sleeping securely in the safety of the invincible, unconquerable, infallible deliverer.

5. No artillery that the enemy hurls at me is effective against me; for I am girded with the armor of grace and favor, which no warrior can penetrate.

6. Although my enemies surround me, yet will I trust in the strength of the arm of my righteous savior; for he is my sole deliverer.

7. My victory is secured in the victor that cannot be defeated.

8. He does not retreat, nor does he falter; but he is steadfast and relentless in his almighty prowess.

9. Jehovah is the name of my God. He is the I Am That I Am God.

10. The fearsome God of Abraham, Isaac and Jacob; the strong arm of Israel, and the deliverer of the Gentiles.

11. His bed is justice, his pillow is power and his blanket is righteousness.

12. He does not sleep or even gets drowsy; his alert-ness is continuous and constant.

13. For he is the only true righteous, almighty living God.

14. Jehovah is flawless and faultless in his ways; and his righteousness is consistent and beyond reproach.

15. The God of my salvation never falters but is pure in his holiness above all others.

16. He is indeed reliable and trustworthy; therefore, I have unwavering assurance and confidence that my God is always able to deliver me according to his purpose.

17. Therefore I will abide in him forever; I will trust in the strength of his almighty arm.

18. I will not cease to praise him and exalt him; for there is no other God like the awesome Jehovah God.

19. In him are my deliverance, my security and my rest. Hallelujah!

Kingdom Psalm 14

The word of the Lord is my daily bread on which I sumptuously feast.

Your word, oh Lord, is spiritual nutrition to my soul and life to my spirit.

2. It is that which my spirit desires to feast on even before the dawning of thy mornings.

3. For even while yet in bed, your word penetrates my head and saturates my thoughts so that my imaginations focus on you.

4. Your word brings your secrets of light out of hiding and presents them before me on a platter.

5. Though your mysteries are numberless O God, you unfold them to those who diligently feast on your word with sincerity of heart and expectation of revelation

6. Through the deep meditation on your word my

thoughts are refreshed daily; my mind is often renewed and my vain imaginations are erased.

7. All unclean thoughts and idle fantasies dissipate like fleeting vapors of smoke.

8. I proclaim in triumph that your word is the fortress of my mind, the defender of my thoughts and the purifier of my imaginations.

9. Often the enemy hurls a barrage of fiery darts at my spirit; but your word rises in my defense.

10. It lies and waits in the storeroom of my heart in great abundance, ready to ambush any evil saboteurs.

11. Like an army of trained warriors, it lies alert, waiting in readiness to defend the seed of your righteousness that you have planted in my heart.

12. For there is a continuous germination of truth taking place within my heart.

13. It flourishes in the fertile foundations of your holy word; it brings forth righteous fruit in my daily life.

14. Even in my moments of uncertainty and doubt, it is your word O God that restores my faith.

15. It is your Holy Spirit that gives me direction and focus; my determination is renewed and my spirit motivated.

16. Your word and your Holy Spirit propel me to press on in spite of the uncertainties and the internal conflicts.

17. They rekindle my determination; they also invigorate my resolve to achieve the standard that you have set for me.

18. When my soul was darkened by ignorance, I basked in the light of your word, which shines like the noonday sun.

19. For therein lie wisdom, knowledge and much understanding.

20. The brilliance of the divine radiance of your word illuminates my spirit and soul and gives sight to my blinded eyes.

21. That is why your word is my daily portions; for there is no other meal so fulfilling.

22. Nor is there anything more nourishing and strengthening.

23. It is indeed from your word that I glean my daily strength to face an evil world.

24. Your word alone is truth, my God; for all other bears false witness.

25. It is indeed with your word that I praise you and glorify you.

26. I cannot live without the life giving power of your holy word.

27. It is my guide in the darkness and my chauffeur in my daily ride.

Kingdom Psalm 15

My praise and my worship are my joy and strength.

My Prayer. Jehovah my Lord and my God; it is your purpose for my life that I pursue with the uttermost diligence; for it is your purpose that I want to be.

2. Deplete me of all self; empty me of my will and purge me of all ulterior motives within my heart.

3. Cleanse me of all spiritual impurities: Then refill me with holiness and godliness so that my living will be a reflection of God.

4. I am nothing without your unmerited grace; even my shortcomings are too many stumbling blocks in my pursuit of righteousness.

5. But you have flooded them all with grace and tempered them with mercy.

6. So because of your love I can now walk circumspectly in righteousness and stand upright in faith.

7. That is why I awake at midnight with a praise in my mouth, and arise at daybreak with a song on my lips and a psalm in my heart.

8. I walk in the glorious sunshine with a heart enlightened with meditation.

9. Even as I drive my vehicle in the confusion of traffic; I whisper to you in prayerful intimacy as your lover.

10. There are not sufficient psalms in my heart, nor are there enough songs in my mouth to praise you.

11. For you O God are worthy of much more praise than we have the capacity to offer you.

12. That is why the seas praise you in their leaping waves, and the trees bow in humble praise.

13. Even so, the birds chirp their praises unto you, and the dogs bark in praise.

14. Therefore my praises are more than empty gestures and my songs are more than mere entertainment.

15. My shout far surpasses carnal excitement and emotions.

16. They are all sincere, heart felt praises and worship to the almighty triune God Jehovah.

17. My praises bring thanksgiving and my worship brings fellowship.

18. For there is absolutely no wholesomeness; nor is there any satisfaction or fulfillment in spirit without praising you oh God Jehovah.

19. When I praise you I come alive in you and you in me; then I dance in your royal courts.

overwhelmed, by spiritual transfiguration.

21. The wicked are the living dead, because they have not sought the fountain of life; therefore, they have not found it.

22. They die daily because they have not received the Messiah; he alone is the giver of life.

23. The wicked do not know him, and therefore are not ready for his second coming.

24. They have not es-teemed his royal highness; nor have they sought refuge in the cross.

25. Unfortunately they have not embraced his resurrection.

26. Nor have they acknowledged the redeeming power of his precious life giving blood that he shed on Calvary.

20. When I worship you, I sit in awe at your holy feet,

27. They are therefore ignorant of the power of the cross and hence, they deem it foolishness.

28. However, to those of us who preach the cross and believe, we have received righteousness and power.

29. It is the blood of Christ on the cross that empowers us to keep the devil at bay.

30. It is the power of the blood that put his demons to flight, for we are able to conquer even the demonic forces that conquer mortal men.

31. The Christ of the cross excites me and gives me the power to praise and the fervor to worship.

32. It is in Christ where praises are birthed, and there-fore I will maintain my abode in the Christ of the cross,

33. Therefore, I will sing his glorious praises for ever-more throughout God's eternity.

34. All praise and glory is yours Oh God.

Kingdom Psalm 16

Jehovah is the awesome God of the universe.

Oh magnificent Jehovah, you are too awesome for comparison and too mind boggling for the human imagination to even attempt to fathom.

2. For your heights are unreachable and your depths are unfathomable.

3. Your light is far too glorious and magnificent to behold in its fullness, even by men while clothed in mortality.

4. Oh Lord, your excellence supercedes the limited scope of man's definition; it is without the bounds of man's vocabulary and outside his realm of knowledge.

5. I know of God; that to you man's wisdom is that of an exalted fool, and his pedestal on which he places him-self is your footstool.

6. To you, man's knowledge is but a snowflake in a raging blizzard.

7. His understanding is but a flicker in a pitch, dark night, searching for a needle in a billion haystacks.

8. How exalted is your name, even beyond and above the moon and the stars.

9. For it is you, O God, that have empowered men with wisdom to penetrate the galaxies and visit the planets.

10. Indeed it's your name that is on their Lips and your praises in their mouths.

11. It is you that are the all inclusive God, independent in your source, complete in your being and righteous in your ways.

12. Yet you have empowered man with dominion over the earth and over all living things.

13. Nevertheless, you have dominion over man; for as the pottery is the product of the potter, so are we the creation of Jehovah.

14. From the beginning we were blessed above the living creatures of the earth.

15. Because we were made in your image and it is your likeness, and it is your breath of life that we breathe in our lungs.

16. For you are the Almighty Jehovah God; but you have deemed us worthy of being little gods.

17. Presently we are aging mortals, but those who are faithful to you will be rewarded with your shroud of immortality and a crown of victory.

18. My God, you have made us so blessed and so privileged.

19. It is a blessing just knowing that the ultimate prize will be beholding your glory face to face.

20. However, what is most gratifying is knowing that I will abide in your glorious presence.

21. For there, time will be transformed into everlasting eternity. Sholaba!

Kingdom Psalm 17

Jehovah is the provider and sustainer of salvation.

Blessed is the recipient of salvation.

2. For in his grasp is an endless bundle of benefits; in his paths are unlimited blessings.

3. But his path is narrow and straight; for there is no room for indecision, hesitation or diversion.

4. It is a one way street with no stop signs and provision for retreat.

5. The recipient of salvation must be vigilant in the pursuit of his treasures, lest they evade him and the thief snatches them from his grasp.

6. He must be consistent in his onward stride and relentless in his commitment to the pursuit of his destiny; for there lay the prize.

7. His salvation is a continuous process through the tunnel of faith.

8. The tunnel is littered with trials and tribulations; but he needs to overcome and endure if he is to reach the finish line.

9. He must persevere if he is to unlock the countless benefits along the way before he gets to the ultimate prize.

10. For holy are his strides and righteous are his exploits along the way.

11. I declare that the provider and preserver of his salvation is the righteous one.

12. He is the author of righteousness.

13. For God is ageless and tireless: He is faithful in all his ways and a deliver of all his promises.

14. He will walk with you if you so desire; he will safely escort you through the flood and through the fire.

15. He will even preserve you through the devastating tsunami.

16. So walk in boldness and righteousness; walk with perseverance and patience.

17. Even through all your trials and conflicts, walk in holiness with all spiritual dignity.

18. Uphold the principles of the heavenly kingdom; falter not in the face of persecution and adversity, but rather rejoice in triumph.

19. Let love radiate from you like the rays of nuclear energy, even toward your sworn enemies.

20. For you are empowered over and above the ordinary man.

21. For the rod and staff of God is in your hand, even as it was in the hand of Moses, his prophet and servant.

22. Be not dismayed because your wilderness awaits you on your journey.

23. It is all staged for your maturation and your promotion.

24. For your wilderness will prune you; and your wilderness will hone you.

25. It is there that your testing awaits you; it is there that your perfection awaits you.

26. Nevertheless, sons of God be comforted; for your wilderness is on the doorstep of your destiny.

27. Endure it with patience and expectation.

Kingdom Psalm 18

My destiny is safe and secured in Jesus the Christ.

I am so delighted to give thanks to you O father God.

2. For yet another day the sun is arisen over my head.

3. Lord, if I had died in sin, I could not behold this miracle today.

4. But you have been merciful yet another time.

5. Lord I am mindful also that I could have been crippled or I could have been blinded.

6. Therefore I am ever grateful; I am satisfied that your grace is forever sufficient for me.

7. Your grace will lead me through the pathway of eternity.

8. Oh Lord my God, you are a beacon of strength: It was worth it all since the day I repented.

9. Mere words cannot explain the power of your love, and man cannot count your blessings that you send us from above.

10. That is why you deserve all the glory and all the praise: because you are God and so much higher are your righteous ways.

11. I will bend my knees and I will lift up holy hands because you confound the wicked and foil their evil plans.

12. I will praise you in song and I'll praise you in dance because you're always in the midst of my circumstance.

13. Oh God my redeemer, my savior, my hope; without your love O Lord, to hell I will go.

14. That's why unto you I have committed my ways, and that's why I will serve you to the end of my days.

15. You're my shield, my buckler, and you are my strong tower. I bask in the glory of your Holy Ghost power.

16. You're my comforter, my redeemer, much closer than a brother, you take me up when I'm forsaken by my father and mother.

17. You're the love of my life, on whom. I can depend; with perfect agape love that I don't even understand.

18. Oh the favor unmerited, the abundance of grace; that's the reason, dear Lord, no one can take your place.

19. I was a sinner, but you saved me from both death and the grave, from condemnation and hell, which is the sinner's wage.

20. Now I'm in heavenly places, by invitation of the King; I'll be singing heavenly songs that even the angels can't sing.

21. Your pour out so many blessings that I don't have room to contain; you pour out your Holy Spirit like the abundant latter rain.

22. I have tasted you Lord, and I have seen that it is good, and you've filled me with power, like you promised you would.

23. So I'm delighted to bless you, on your heavenly throne because you saved me from sin and you made me your own.

24. What more can I ask for, you have prepared me a place; a new earth and new heaven, where my destiny is safe. Sholaba!

Kingdom Psalm 19

Troubles do not endure with the righteous; for Jehovah is their God.

Consider my plight O Lord; for a multitude of troubles follow me in hot pursuit.

2. I am to trouble as fish is to flies, and they easily overtake me.

3. Behold they attempt to strangle me all day long.

4. My troubles multiply like sand in a sandstorm; why Lord do they constantly seek to consume me?

5. Why Lord do they buffet me about like a football?

6. For even my pillow brings me no relief; I toss and turn all through the night like a ship caught in a violent storm.

7. My dreams are plagued with perplexity at night; my imaginations are fraught with anxiety by day.

8. My cupboards suffer lack as if they were rare sacked, and my refrigerator is often bare like a cold desert.

9. My heart is often heavy with stress and my eyes are filled with sorrow tears because my children stomachs growl with hunger pangs.

10. I am often broke in my pockets and broke in my spirit; depression takes a strong hold of me.

11. As I sit in bewilderment, my thoughts betray me and tell me there is no help available.

12. They secretly whisper in my ear that there is no rescue and there is no solace available for me.

13. It is then O Lord that I remember that you promised never to leave me nor forsake me; that when my mother and father forsake me, you will come to my rescue.

14. It is at that stressful time that I vividly recall that the entire earth is yours and also its fullness.

15. Then my sorrowful, pleading cry goes out to you in sincerity; and with a heavy, broken and contrite heart, I humbly bow to you on bending knees.

16. I call on your mighty name in prayer and supplication; and though I am perplexed, I still give you thanks and praises.

17. Like a faithful father to a child, you hear me, you answer me, and you deliver me.

18. My God I am living proof that you are a deliverer; I can testify on the mountaintop that you are a provider.

19. On worldwide television and on the radio waves, I can jubilantly declare your goodness to the nations of the world.

20. For no one else is like you; you are too awesome for comparison.

21. Because you are so mighty in your ways it is impossible for you to be duplicated.

22. For not only do you stand alone, but you stand apart as the Almighty God of the ages.

23. You stand as the God of all creation, the everlasting God and the God of eternity.

24. It is you O Jehovah God that delivers me from my lack and relieves me from my want.

25. I will always lift you up in exaltation because you know how to deliver, and you are an on time God.

Kingdom Psalm 20

The earth is evil and corrupt, but Jehovah shall prevail in righteousness.

Why, O Lord, is the heathen on such a rampage?

2. They follow hard after evil, vanity and debauchery.

3. Their minds are to-tally corrupt, and they possess an evil and rebellious spirit consistently.

4. Why O Lord do they find so much pleasure in the abominable things?

5. They delight in the things that you hate and in the things that you have cursed.

6. Why O Lord do they indulge in such lewd and sadistic acts that send a stench up your nostrils?

7. O how they provoke you to anger, and how they presumptuously kindle your fury.

8. They have saturated the earth with their promiscuous filth; they have infested it with their fornication and folly.

9. Even your sacred institutions of marriage and the family are blatantly desecrated in the public's eye.

10. Their sin is open and presumptuous, and their rebellion is arrogant and disrespectful.

11. For even though you have specifically condemned homosexuality, it is rampant throughout the land.

12. So much so, it has infested your church and dis-graced your sacred order.

13. Those that indulge in this atrocity have even been ordained as shepherds in your sanctuaries, as holy priests, in defiance of your word.

14. They continuously desecrate your house of worship.

15. They defile your holy temples daily; for the bodies of the saints are your temples; therefore, they are consumed with corruption.

16. Lord even marriage, your first institution; that too has been defiled.

17. Now man and man, and woman and woman, are being joined together in unholy matrimony.

18. There is no more fear in the hearts of men today toward their creator.

19. For the sinful acts of the heathen today have far surpassed those of Sodom and Gomorra of yesterday.

20. The stench of their sin is an offence to your nostrils; it is an assault on your holiness.

21. Even bestiality O Lord is often blatantly and shamelessly displayed in cyberspace.

22. They find sexual plea-sure lying with the dumb creatures.

23. For even from the beginning you have demonstrated that the beasts of the field were not fit for a helpmate for Adam.

24. Yet even the dogs they kiss; they mate with them seeking sexual pleasures.

25. They are shameless and are no longer discreet in their vile acts; for they have no fear.

26. Everywhere one turns, pornography is visible; it is openly displayed on the television screens and on the pages of magazines.

27. My God, my God, how much longer will you be long suffering? How long, O God, will you tarry?

28. The entire earth has become morally bankrupt and spiritually polluted.

29. Men have put aside your statutes and have established their own standards of morality.

30. They have ceased to seek your face and have ceased to seek counsel from the anointed lips of your prophets.

31. Instead, they have turned to witchcraft and sorcery.

32. In fact they have out-right rejected your righteous ways and your just counsel.

33. Moreover, they have enlisted the help of all sorts of familiar spirits and ungodly principalities and powers.

34. How long oh Lord will you tarry? How long is your longsuffering? For too much wickedness already abounds in the earth.

35. But the wicked will face harsh judgment, and his condemnation will be intolerable yet eternal.

36. I declare that swift judgment will consume him if he persists to indulge in his immorality and his wickedness.

37. He will face swift rejection in the judgment and reap due grievous recompense.

38. Hear me Oh God, with my cry of mercy, and preserve us your saints from the polluting influences of their evil pleasures.

39. We commit to your holiness, your purity and your sanctification.

40. My God Jehovah, we give total commitment to your righteousness.

41. Because we know the Christ that lives within us is greater than the devil that is going to and from the earth, seeking our souls.

42. We are set apart and sanctified; we are rooted and grounded in truth, and your word is truth, O Christ!

43. We are not in the least doubtful or wavering, but we shall be saved.

44. Because we are stead-fast and unmovable and we decree and declare that we shall endure to the very end.

45. Reign forever Oh God! Reign in righteousness.

46. Nothing will impede your righteousness or stem the flow of your power.

47. For the entire universe is yours, and we your saints are your righteous subjects.

48. We will keep your ways alive in the earth, so that our ways will be pleas-ing to you.

49. Reign forever Oh Lord! Reign in righteousness.

50. For you have created all creation, and you oh God are the endless source of its sustenance.

51. Your reign is eternal and your will shall be done in all the earth, same as it is in heaven.

52. I find comfort and peace in the knowledge that you reign supreme, and you reign righteously.

53. To you oh righteous God, be praise, glory and honor, for evermore. Amen.

PART THREE

Kingdom Psalm 21

Self-righteousness is haughty and a reproach unto God.

Oh wanton man, why do you trust in yourself? Why do you deem yourself righteous? Do you not know that self-righteousness is a sin?

2. How have you become so erroneous in your judgment and so distorted in your convictions?

3. For what reason have you become so puffed up with haughtiness?

4. I dare ask you, who has ordained and anointed you God?

5. For there is but one God who is manifested in the Father, Son and Holy Ghost. Hallelujah!

6. For it is he alone that is complete unto himself; for he alone is almighty and reigns supreme over all gods.

7. Moreover, every divine ordination and anointing are his and his alone; there is no other being in heaven in earth or beneath the earth that is so empowered.

8. Yet you are consumed by your folly and deceived by your humanistic abilities:

9. But even those abilities were given to you by the Almighty God; therefore, honor him for who he really is.

10. O foolish men, everyone needs to be redeemed except God, for he is the redeemer.

11. He needs no redemption, nor does he need any approval. His words need no confirmation by man; for his word is divine truth.

12. He is God in complete-ness and wholesomeness; he is the source.

13. But the fool who says in his heart that he is empowered of himself, and is guided by his intellect is indeed blind and misguided.

14. He who is convinced that the power of his knowledge and his academic prowess is enough to bring him fullness of life; he is misguided by leaning on his own understanding.

15. While the fool says in his heart there is no God, the wise says that in his heart is the Almighty God.

16. For there is a man whose fate is sealed by God and whose future is everlasting abundant life.

17. Therefore, let your academic prowess, your knowledge, and your intellect guide you to the source, for that is true wisdom.

18. Then you can boast of power, ability, wholesomeness and invincibility; for your end will only be your beginning.

19. O conceited man, deliver yourself into the hands of the Almighty God; for therein lies your eternal security.

Kingdom Psalm 22

Your pilgrimage is a road test to prove the excellence of your spiritual mileage.

I do declare that I shall not be moved by the spiritual turbulence and the constant tribulations of this life.

2. For they are nothing more than a heavenly prescribed element of my pilgrimage.

3. Be comforted my brethren; for they are no more than a residual consequence of Adam's disobedience to his creator and our God.

4. For my pilgrimage with men on this earth is only transitory; but my heritage is eternal with God.

5. Therefore, I entreat you my dear saints that you faint not in your righteousness.

6. For time passes as a vapor, but eternity is timeless and everlasting.

7. I admonish you to be diligent in the things of God and to persevere through all trials in steadfastness.

8. For trials are sent to perfect your faith and hone your Christian stature.

9. So be it known that perfection is the result of intense testing.

10. Be aware, saints, that your challenges are not sent to beset you, but rather to perfect you.

11. Therefore, embrace them as an examination to prove your spiritual excellence, and indeed to establish your qualification in patience.

12. For I will embrace my pilgrimage as my battleground, and therefore, be a good soldier for Christ.

13. Through salvation he has equipped me with the whole armor of God.

14. Therefore, I can stand valiantly and victoriously in battle; and I can endure on the battlefield.

15. In fact, I can endure even the test of time; for soon and very soon time will be no more; but God is timeless.

16. I glory in the father's preordained plans; for when my timed pilgrimage is ended, my eternity will just begin.

17. Then will I see my God face to face; I will dwell in his courts and bask in his glorious presence.

18. For the test of my pilgrimage would be worth it all, and the fruit of my patience would be sweet and fulfilling.

19. So as for now, while my pilgrimage is in progress, I will praise my God at all times and honor his righteous statutes unconditionally.

20. I know that he is able to lead me and guide me through the myriad of trials and tribulations.

21. Even until my pilgrimage is over and done with and successfully completed.

22. Praise the almighty name of God.

Kingdom Psalm 23

Be not proud and boastful, but let agape love be your Christian insignia.

23. For he is my sustainer and keeper until my pilgrim-age is over, and until eternity rolls out and time is no more.

Pride is a poison and haughtiness a cancer; many unwary men and women are thereby destroyed.

2. These deadly infections often offer only deception, a pseudo sense of being, and a perception of inflated self worth.

3. Our true worth is really established by Jehovah God and manifested in godliness and humility of character.

4. Children of God be not deceived; for our worth is only as great as our love for one another; for thereby is the yardstick by which it is measured.

5. Let not deceit and conceit pollute your judgment; for it will convince you of false pride and self worth that is only counterfeit.

6. So be wary of pride, conceit and haughtiness; they will fail you in your time of testing.

7. For they themselves are void of worth; they are nothing more than a hollow dream.

8. Let agape love be your true insignia; for it is authentic and will stand the test of time and worthiness.

9. Furthermore, true love is endearing; it will bring you worthy friends who will in turn find you worthy.

10. This would not be haughtiness and conceit in your own heart; but rather authentic accolades of your worth from the sincere hearts of others.

11. So be not boastful of yourself; but give place to love and kind deeds, and also to the uplifting of others.

12. In so doing, you your-self will be lifted up, and your worth and integrity will shine forth effortlessly.

Kingdom Psalm 24

Praise God in faith always, in spite of the prevailing circumstances.

Who will magnify the Lord with me in times of tumult and moments of trouble?

2. Who will raise the banner of triumph with me and give the shout of victory when the battle seems lost?

3. For faith is invisible only to the natural eye, but crystal clear to the spiritual eye that is of God.

4. Through a lack of faith, the children of God have lost many wars that were already won; the enemies were already delivered into their hand.

5. They have indeed also forfeited many accomplished victories and traded their divine triumphs for defeat.

6. It is because their faith lacks vision; therefore, they cannot see the manifested desired result.

7. For faith is only faith when it has been tested and tried in hope; otherwise it is but a vain carnal wish or a mere fleshly desire.

8. Faith comes by hearing, but who will listen even to the authentic word of God when his multitude of troubles seems insurmountable?

9. We look with our eyes and not our spirit; for even the blind man clearly saw his deliverance by Christ and through Christ.

10. He saw without visual sight, and believed without intellectual carnal knowledge.

11. So by faith as small as a grain of mustard seed, we can move mountains and an entire forest of mustard trees.

12. God in his gracious-ness has given us all a measure of faith that he may be glorified.

13. Then the question still prevails: will Christ find faith in the earth when he comes?

14. Only if in faith we exercise the measure that he has given us, and if we build on that measure daily in prayer and supplication.

15. Because if we are going to please God, we must have faith; otherwise we cannot please him.

Kingdom Psalm 25

Continually guard your minds against evil thoughts; let your meditation be righteous.

Bridle your imaginations or they will go astray, and you are soon to follow.

2. For wild imaginations is a breeding ground for lewd and vile acts.

3. It is no secret that ungodly fantasies, once left unchecked, inevitably lead to ungodly acts.

4. For the mind is fertile and vulnerable when it does not host the Holy Spirit of God, and when it does not yield to him in total submission.

5. Then there is no door-keeper, nor is there censor-ship; for the Holy Spirit is an impenetrable defense, and even an effective repel-lent against the infiltration of evil.

6. For the carnal mind is susceptible to invasion by evil thoughts; they appear fully laced with seductive enticement.

7. Once left unchallenged, they reproduce and multiply like amoeba.

8. They feed and strive on the nakedness of your unguarded mind; therefore, your mind needs to be clothed with the Holy Spirit of God.

9. For this reason, the mind needs to be regenerated in newness daily; in holy new-ness, which the Holy Spirit will accomplish if given the chance.

10. The master of evil knows when there is no safe-guard and no holy protection on your mind; he knows when there is an open invitation for evil thoughts.

11. So therefore, meditate on the word of God day and night; it is a shield against the onslaught of evil thoughts.

12. Pray without ceasing; for the fervent prayer of the righteous prevails over much evil.

13. Sing holy songs and psalms; even in your heart; they too are a repellent to evil thoughts.

14. Stand on godly truths and declarations; for greater is Christ that is in you, than Satan that is without.

15. You are a son of God oh saint. The enemy has absolutely no dominion over you or your mind, for it is also the temple of God.

16. The temple of God is holy, and therefore, the thoughts that generate inside ought also to be holy.

17. For the life you live is a manifestation of the thoughts you think; so in order to live righteous, you must first think righteous thoughts.

18. So saints of God, purge your minds and saturate them with righteous thoughts, leaving no room for unrighteous thoughts to creep in.

19. For the mind is a terrible thing to contaminate and desecrate; once desecrated, it puts the entire body and soul to waste.

20. Therefore, let our thoughts and imaginations be pure and holy.

21. Then our lives would be a reflection of the same; and we would live holy and acceptable to our holy God.

Kingdom Psalm 26

No man has light or sight except he has Christ.

Observe the sinner as he sleeps; for even his sunlit days are darkened by evil.

2. His eyes are wide open yet he is asleep; for he is not 9. awake to righteousness.

3. Nor does he see the Kingdom; for he is not born again, therefore his eyes are blinded.

4. He is therefore headed for the dark pit of hell, for he is spritually blind and is being led by eyes that are also blinded.

5. His state is sad; it is continual blindness and dark-ness, for in him there is no light, nor does he have any sight.

6. However, the saints are the light of the world. In them there is no darkness, for they are children of vision.

7. While they too were once blind, they now see, even without sight in their eyes.

8. For whosoever is still blind and is asleep in dark-ness, awake while Christ calls you, for he is the light that lightens every man.

9. There is no man that has light or sight without Christ; but only blindness and perpetual darkness.

Kingdom Psalm 27

The stench of sin in the congregations of the Lord is rancid in his nostrils.

Righteous saints of God, mourn continuously and solemnly for the congregations.

2. Let your hearts be broken and contrite as you beseech your holy God on their behalf.

3. For sin, corruption and wickedness have infiltrated the Christian congregations; even the desecrated pulpits creak from the assault of evil.

4. Though sackcloth and ashes and the renting of garments have been done away with, let your supplication be earnest and steadfast, and rent your hearts in the spirit of repentance.

5. Get down on your face prostrate and cry out to God; for the stench of sin in the congregations of the Lord is rancid in his nostrils.

6. Let us pray earnestly and fervently for forgiveness, for mercy and for sanctification.

7. Let us make an honest heart felt appeal to God that he would stay his terrible hand of vengeance while the rebellious ones kindle his anger.

8. For the congregations of the denominations are testing the mighty hand of God; they are tempting him sorely.

9. His longsuffering nature is being exploited and abused; his unmerited favor toward us is being taken for granted.

10. Who has taken note of the signs of the times that are all around us?

11. Have the severe hurricanes that have recently ravaged the islands and Florida gone unnoticed?

12. Have the congregations given blinded eyes to the tsunami that has devastated the Asian nations?

13. Are the earthquakes in diverse places not recognized by the saints of God as the hand of God at work, even according to his promised word?

14. Are his prophetic words in his holy scriptures ignored and counted for naught?

15. Why do the congregations tempt God presumptuously? Isn't his wrath sufficiently kindled against them for their persistent unrighteousness that they have already committed?

16. Are the devastating floods and landslides in Hispaniola, in America and else-where not fulfillment of the prophetic scriptures?

17. Why do the saints behave like the heathens and like heretics and reproach the holy God?

18. For his name is being disgraced by those that are called by his name and profess Christianity even more so than by the heathen.

19. Have the congregations forgotten that he is a jealous God, and that he is a just God who abhors wrong and punishes wrongdoers?

20. Does not the word of God state that judgment will begin in the house of the Lord? Are we therefore provoking God to hasten that judgment?

21. Let us declare an era of sanctification; for revival is needed for the congregations of the Lord and not for the world.

22. For he that is dead needs to be born again, but he that is asleep and dying needs to be revived again.

23. For as sons of God, we aught not to bring reproach to his impeccable name and desecration to his living temples.

24. Vengeance is mine, said the Lord; I will repay. So let us not any longer tempt him to dish out such terrible repayment.

25. For it will not be pleas-ant, nor will it be tolerable; the wrath of God is terrible and his vengeance is devastating.

Kingdom Psalm 28

The heart is the source of all intents, be they good or bad.

The Lord Jesus the Christ is so near to be so far away from the hearts of so many of God's people.

2. Yet they say that they love God; but it is indeed a farce and only lip service.

3. Their lips only are committed to their words, but their hearts are commit-ted only to the Son of Perdition and to serving him.

4. They worship Christ only with vain verbal expression and confused emotions, but they have no relationship.

5. Their worship is rhetorical and traditional, but they have no fellowship.

6. For light has no relationship with darkness whatsoever, and unrighteousness has no fellowship with righteousness.

7. But the wheat and the tares will grow together; some will bare fruit and some will be unfruitful.

8. However, on the day of harvest and at the appointed hour of reckoning, they shall be separated.

9. There will be very much disappointment on that day; for all those who have deceived themselves shall be exposed. They shall be openly rejected and ushered through the portals of a miserable and fiery hell.

10. But those who have intimately loved Christ with their hearts and not their lips, they shall be gloriously received by Christ with welcoming arms, and shall be rewarded bountifully and abundantly.

11. Both the good and the bad shall all reap what they have sown with their hearts; for that is the source of sincere intents for both good and evil.

12. Therefore, you sons and daughters of men; render your hearts to Christ and not your lips; for your vain words do not move the Spirit of God on your behalf.

13. Hear me children, lip service is futile if the heart has not purposed it; it therefore finds no honor with God.

Kingdom Psalm 29

Zion is the holy city of God; there will he abide with his elect.

The gates of Zion will definitely not be opened to dogs, sorcerers, whore-mongers and the likes; but only the righteous shall enter.

2. The defiled has no place in Zion, for Zion is the holy city of God. It is pure and undefiled.

3. God himself shall dwell in Zion; he and the Lamb shall abide with the sons of God and the elect of God.

4. For his very presence shall glorify the city and shall give it light.

5. There will be no sun and no moon in that glorious city, for their light will not be needed in the holy city of Zion.

6. Finally my friends, God will dwell with men and men with God.

7. No form of evil may enter the portals of Zion, for it is holy and unpolluted. It is reserved for holiness only and for those that are holy.

8. Let the redeemed of the Lord remain faithful; let them be spotless and blame-less; then will Zion be their inheritance; then will Zion be their place of eternal refuge and their sanctuary of worship.

Kingdom Psalm 30

Who is man in the divine sight of God?

Who am I O Lord? A mere mortal robed in sinful flesh that you have predestined to be conformed into the image 8. of your holy son?

2. Who am I that even before the foundation of the world, you had slain the perfect, impeccable, sinless Lamb, even for my sins?

3. Why is it that you have always been so mindful, so concerned and so caring for man?

4. Man is so expandable, so volatile, so undependable, yet you have ordained us to be your sons.

5. What is it O God? Reveal the concealed mystery; for you have established man as the curator of every living being.

6. Who is this one called man that you have given him power and dominion over all of the earth?

7. That you have put all other living creatures under his authority and made them subject and submissive to him?

8. Even after disobeying you and serving your arch-enemy the son of perdition, you have shown grace and mercy.

9. Being the divine and wise God that you are, you were cognizant of our failure even before we failed you.

10. Yet you had already initiated a salvation plan; yet you had already put in place a plan of restoration.

11. In spite of our foolish choice, you refused to let us die the death that Adam has chosen for us in the garden.

12. Instead, you have sent your righteous, most holy, only begotten son, from the sanctity of his utopian abode in heaven, to die for us.

13. It was so that we may have yet another unmerited chance to live righteously and eternally;

14. And that we may have yet another choice, to choose between eternal life and death, light and darkness and between good and evil.

15. Who has proven more undeserving than man? Yet you have invented grace to be administered when your goodness and mercy are unmerited by man.

16. Rather the question is who are you O God, most magnificent, most holy, most righteous, most excellent and most forgiving?

17 In your incomparable, perfect love, you alone have given longsuffering a meaning that man cannot achieve; but only you.

18. Yet you qualify our steadfastness, patience and commitment; them you have deemed as longsuffering.

19. It is you O Jehovah that is the mystery, whose ways are beyond comprehension.

20. For you have chosen man at your will to fellow-ship with you and to live and reign with you.

21. It is you O God, who are an awesome God.

22. All glory, praise, honor and majesty are yours forever and ever. Amen.

PART FOUR

Kingdom Psalm 31

Bless God in song and dance; for God has created them for his pleasure.

Let your soul dance in delight of the music, and let your spirit rejoice in the melody of holiness.

2. Sing merry songs of dance and praise, and let God find pleasure in your rhythms.

3. Let your renditions emanate from a spiritual heart; then would your music be heavenly and your songs praiseful.

4. Even in the heavenly courts of Jehovah is singing and dancing.

5. For God has created it for his pleasure.

6. Moreover, in the vocal chords of Lucifer he had made instruments of music.

7. For God had created it for his pleasure; indeed for his praise and for his worship.

8. So let your lyrics magnify God in his holy place and glorify him on his throne.

9. May they speak of his goodness and tell of his good gifts toward the children of men.

10. Boast of his multitude of blessings; they are numberless as the dust particles in the deserts and boast openly of your many promotions by him.

11. Remind him in appreciation of his favor that he freely bestowed upon you, both in his eyes and even in the eyes of your enemies.

12. Sing prayerful choruses that glorify his name and exalt him in his magnificent glory.

13. Let six stringed guitars, the bass guitar and synthesizers harmonize with the horns and synchronize with the drums.

14. So that the music will be rich in harmony and endearing and worshipful in the ears of God.

15. Have the holy voices chorale in melodious harmony, for then even the Holy Spirit of God would be invoked.

16. Let us dance the dances of praise in the shuffling of the feet, also in the choreography of hands and the movement of body,

17. All to the glory and honor of the Almighty God.

18. Blessed be the name of the Holy God of Zion in song and dance; they are a fitting tribute of praise and worship to him.

Kingdom Psalm 32

Let your boasting be on the name of Jehovah; he is the source and man is a mere facilitator.

Who can boast of holiness except he boasts of grace?

2. Who can boast of grace except he boasts of Christ?

3. Who can boast of Christ except he boasts of Jehovah?

4. For only Jehovah is God Almighty. It is he that reigns supreme in the heavens, even over the earth.

5. The dominion of God is without boundaries, and its universal sphere is limitless.

6. They are all his creations and the incredible craft of his mighty hands.

7. For the very first and most awesome wonder of the world is Jehovah; even the world itself is a wonder of the world.

8. All boasting can only be by God; he is the source and man is but a mere facilitator.

9. Therefore, let our boasting be in the Lord and of the Lord; moreover, let humility be found in our spirit.

10. Let our boasting be in acknowledgement of God as Jehovah and of his mighty, incredible and awesome prowess.

11. For man has nothing good of himself to boast about because when left to his own devices, he is evil in his heart continuously.

12. Therefore, I make my boast in the Lord, for he alone is good and pleasant.

13. For only the goodness of the Lord can I depend on anytime and all the time.

14. Bless the Lord for his unwavering goodness; in him I make my boast publicly.

Kingdom Psalm 33

Who is worthy of praise except the Almighty God?

Who is it that is mortal and worthy of praise?

2. Which mortal is there that is capable of any works worthy of praise except his works be of God?

3. For any acts worthy of praise are acts of God; he alone is worthy of praise.

4. Moreover, every creature that has been created is created by the supreme and Almighty God.

Kingdom Psalm 34

The gates of hell cannot prevail against the redeemed of the Lord.

Hallelujah is my praise; I declare that the gates of hell cannot prevail against me.

2. For they are damned, and so are those that sit in them.

3. Behold, they are all snare setters and plotters.

4. Their plots are devious and their snares are of deadly intents.

5. However, there is absolutely no prosperity in their plots against me; their snares entrap their own evil feet.

6. For I am enveloped in divine protection, and my protector is aware of all malicious secret intents formed against me:

7. Even so, he is able to foil every devious and evil plot that is formed against his redeemed.

8. In him is my rest; that rest is secured in holiness and kept in power and might from heaven above.

9. My safety is divinely secure and cannot be breached. Neither can it ever be overcome; nor can it be destroyed. For it is of God.

10. So let the wicked plotters hatch their treacherous plots, and the evil snare setters set their devious snares.

11. For the ditches they dig await their speedy arrival with a resounding, destructive welcome.

12. They will be engulfed and consumed by evil fires from their own ditches and caught in their own snares:

13. But I can afford to boast in deliverance, because my deliverer is none other than the great God of Zion.

14. He will live forever, he will endure forever, and he will reign forever and ever and beyond all eternity.

15 So hallelujah is my praise. Sholaba.

Kingdom Psalm 35

The potency of the prescription for your sin lies in the precious blood of Christ.

Jesus the Christ is the illuminator of men's hearts and the eliminator of their sins.

2. There is no light in him, except there is Christ in him, for Jesus is the redemptive light.

3. Everyman that does not have Christ is indeed in darkness and cannot find his way.

4. His path is cluttered with sin and littered with iniquity; his deeds are a stumbling block and his imaginations a hurdle before him.

5. Even his advances are retrogressive and calamitous; his achievements are liabilities unto himself.

6. He is drunken by the wine of ignorance and infested and infected by the virus of sin.

7. His cure does not lie in the skilled hands of a mortal physician; nor does his rehabilitation rest in the professional counseling of an ungodly psychiatrist.

8. For the potency of his prescription lies in the precious blood of Jesus Christ.

9. Therein lie his redemption and his salvation, and there is no other source of remedy.

10. For Jesus the Christ is even the great physician; he is able to heal mind, body and soul.

11. Therefore, let men submit himself to the Messiah who is able to do all things, for he is Lord of all.

Kingdom Psalm 36

I need my needs to be filled according to God's abundant, limitless riches in glory.

I want my needs to be filled; however, my wants stand in the way.

2. But I want my needs to be filled; I need my soul fed because it hungers and thirsts for holiness.

3. I want my needs to be filled; I need the power of God manifested in my life in my daily walk.

4. I want my needs to be filled; I need to let my light shine before the entire world and glorify God in the process.

5. I want my needs to be filled; I need to resist the wiles of the devil all day and all night long, even in my dreams.

6. I want my needs to be filled; I need to be filled with the Holy Ghost and live and move under the anointing of the Almighty God.

7. I want my needs to be filled; I need the strength to love my enemy, bless those that curse me and pray for them who spitefully use me.

8. I want my needs to be filled; I need to be able to stand on the promises of God, even in the face of adversity; for Christ who is on the inside of me is greater than Satan that is without.

9. I want my needs to be filled; I need the commitment to pray without ceasing, for the fervent prayer of the righteous gets a multitude of results.

10. I want my needs to be filled; I need the obedience to allow God to order my footsteps, for he will lead me in the path of righteousness always.

11. I want my needs to be filled; I need the faith to allow you to supply all my needs according to your riches in glory; for you are rich in houses, land, bullion and the gifts of the Spirit.

12. For you are my God, and in you do I put my trust unconditionally; therefore, I will never ever be confounded. Hallelujah!

Kingdom Psalm 37

Faith will gain you salvation, but without works you will be fruitless.

I believe in my faith that Jesus the Christ is Lord; I have confidence therein.

2. Therefore, he showed me grace and freely gave me salvation because of my repentance.

3. I could not earn it, nor could I perform any kind of deeds to merit it as a deserving reward; for it is a priceless gift from God through Christ.

4. My performance in love and in obedience to Christ and my execution of righteous works: They are what me earn rewards; unimaginable rewards in the Kingdom of heaven. They earn me stars in my crown

5. For once saved by unmerited grace, then my works accrue interests of great and precious rewards from God.

6. It is by my works of love that I will be evaluated and graded; hence, I strive to reach the acceptable standard of God.

7. I have little or no regard for man's standard; but it is God's standard that I endeavor to achieve.

8. For God's standard is higher, and God's standard is holy and surpasses that of the righteousness of man.

9. Therefore may the saints of God work.while it is yet day; for you Gentiles, even your season will come to an end.

10. Execute good and righteous deeds; they will gain you rewards and promotions even in heaven way beyond what men may give.

11. For faith is good for salvation; but faith without performance will be fruitless to the redeemed saints.

12. The saints must therefore move in faith and work in faith; for therein is your steady and progressive advancement in Jesus Christ.

Kingdom Psalm 38

The backslider is misled by his carnal mind and held captive by the fleshy desires that burn in his loins.

My soul travails in pain when the presumptuous backslider rejoices in his erring ways.

2. I am astounded that he is able to again find satisfaction in sin and comfort in transgression.

3. How is it that he becomes fonder of Satan than of God; moreover, how is he able to reject God and accept the devil?

4. For after feasting on righteousness and basking in grace, how is unrighteous-ness preferred? How is hate preferred over grace and love?

5. I fail to understand how death becomes more attractive than eternal life, and eternal torment more desirable than joyful abundant life.

6. Therefore, the conclusion of the matter is that man is a fool and his thoughts convoluted.

7. He is blinded by the distortion of his very own understanding; his carnal imaginations are vile and indeed perverted.

8. He is misled by his own mind and held captive by the fleshy desires that burn in his loins.

9. So the backslider is an arrogant fool; he has never totally surrendered to the Holy Spirit of God; for his walk is still in pursuit of the flesh.

10. His mind was never renewed and is therefore still excited by the things of the flesh, after which he longs.

11. So let the children of God be sanctified by the word of God and baptized in the Holy Spirit of God.

12. Let us walk continuously and steadfastly in the grace and deliverance afforded us through the blood of Jesus Christ.

Kingdom Psalm 39

Allow the spirit of God to execute authority over your flesh and bring it under submission.

The fool dances to the music of sin and sings to the tune of vanity.

2. He has an appetite for sin that leaves a residual bitter taste in his mouth, yet he savors it delightfully.

3. The error of his choices are disguised by his lustful desires that rage in his sinful flesh.

4. For the flesh is corrupt and persuasive simply because it is untamed and unrestrained by the spirit.

5. Therefore, his spirit is submissive to his corrupted flesh; he continuously pursues after vanity.

6. He craves to fulfill the desires of his flesh and is led astray by his own cravings.

7. The flesh is devious and misleading in its ungodly desires. If left unchecked, it will consume the mind, body and soul.

8. Therefore, allow the spirit of God to execute authority over your flesh and bring it under godly submission.

9. Then will your desires be transformed and your ways please God.

10. Then will your deliverance be assured and your life preserved for the Kingdom of God.

11. For no spirit should glory in untamed flesh, but 4. rather the flesh should glory in a righteous spirit.

Kingdom Psalm 40

Dwell always in the presence of the Lord and in his sanctuary; therein is his anointing.

Jehovah, how I love to dwell in your sanctuary: therein is the anointing in abundance.

2. Therein is glory and serene tranquility; therein also is a Spirit of benevolence.

3. Lord your holy presence alone is imposing, potent and inspiring; it overshadows me.

4. Your glorious presence O Lord, consumes, enlivens and anoints; it also empowers and enlightens my mind and enriches my spirit.

5. Your anointing opens blinded eyes and exposes concealed revelations and reveals hidden mysteries.

6. Your presence is so awesome and your glory so magnificent; only you O Lord are so marvelous.

7. I am transformed in your presence and renewed by your anointing; I am made brand new in spirit.

8. You deem me worthy to be privileged of being in your sacred presence and of fellowshipping with you in your royal courts.

9. For only the redeemed and the esteemed of the Lord are afforded such divine privileges.

10. Only the dead in Christ, who is therefore alive in Christ, is counted worthy of such heavenly honor.

11. Therefore, I will not relinquish or forfeit my righteous heritage by dancing with the devil in the courts of hell.

12. But rather I will abide in the sanctity of holiness under the wings of the almighty God forever and ever. Amen.

PART FIVE

Kingdom Psalm 41

God's anointing brings his written word well alive with miraculous power and might.

Your anointing is awesome O Lord; it is so powerful and so miraculous.

2. It brings your printed word alive and it speaks in eloquent silence from the pages of your holy Bible.

3. Your precious word gives your directives to the very soul of man and pro-vides food and sustenance to his spirit.

4. O how invigorating is your word and how enlightening are your precepts.

5. For it is like a cloud by day and a pillar of fire by night as it righteously directs my footsteps continuously.

6. It is a floodlight to my darkened paths; it is as smooth, hard asphalt to my rough and rugged roads.

7. Your word O Lord is a comfort to me in my hour of distress and a solace in my time of bereavement.

8. It is powerful in counsel; it is mighty in deliverance, yet it is swift in rebuke and chastening.

9. The power and might of your word is way beyond description.

10. Indeed its multiplicity of abilities exceeds comprehension even to the mortal mind of man.

11. Therefore, your word is my divine counsel and my royal decree.

12. For you O God are holy and righteous, and your word alone is undisputable truth. Sholaba.

Kingdom Psalm 42

May the saints of God pursue the voice of God with an attentive ear and a willing and obedient heart.

Who will know the voice of the Lord when he calls out to his saints?

2. Indeed, who is spiritually positioned to hear the voice of the good shepherd?

3. Or is he yet another voice crying in the wilder-ness of sin, for even saints seem deaf to his appeal.

4. Their ears are deafened with rebellion and numbed by self-will; they have been consumed by their own agendas.

5. O God have mercy; for even some that hear listen with an inattentive and dis-obedient ear and an indifferent spirit

6. For they have allowed sin to divert their attention away from you.

7. In their wayward frolicking they have allowed transgression to diminish the desire and longing to hear your sweet voice.

8. Who will turn back their ears to hear the voice of the Lord; who will respond in willingness to heed his cry?

9. O ye Gentiles, your season is winding down and your era-unmerited favor is coming to a close; be aware that even your day of reckoning is at hand.

10. You were bought with the holy, royal blood of Jesus Christ; will you not walk in royalty? Will you not stand in righteousness?

11. Or will you persist in the daily crucifixion of the Son of God? Will you forfeit your heavenly heritage for the love of sin?

12. Your ears are tickled with the vibes of ungodliness, and your hearts are delighted in they ways of death.

13. Let the redeemed of the Lord live in holy liberty; let the saints of God pursue the voice of God with an attentive ear and a willing and obedient heart.

14. For the joy of the Lord assures the completion of our salvation and the fulfillment of our heavenly heritage.

Kingdom Psalm 43

Let him that refutes God be silenced, ashamed and confounded. As for me, I will submit to the almighty voice of Jehovah.

Lord you are a mystery and your ways mysterious.

2. No one can fathom your ways until you reveal your ways to him.

3. I am never daunted by the adversaries and the critics or depressed by their ranting and raging because they do not comprehend your purpose for my life.

4. They all oppose and fight vigilantly against me because they are ignorant of your plans; so they operate on feelings and heed knowledge.

5. They have rejected me; yea, they even despise me and have counted me out; they have declared me the underdog.

6. But I am not troubled or anxious; I am not confused or disheartened, for I am doing your bidding.

7. Neither am I con-founded because I am responding to your call in dutiful obedience.

8. So I will bide my time in faith; I will stay my course in hope, because your will always prevails.

9. Even if I fail to succeed in my timing, I will neither falter, nor will I be disheartened; because your timing alone is perfect timing.

10. Therefore, I will endure their criticism and the rash, abrasive and abusive words and will laugh at their venomous condemnation.

11. I will smile even at their castigation. Because it is you O Jehovah that is God; there is no mortal that can usurp your seat of authority.

12. It is you that will have the last laugh; it is I that will prevail because of my obedience and subjection to your will.

13. My faith and my diligence will pay off; for it is in you that I have my trust.

14. So I am courageous in my steadfastness and humble in my demeanor, for only you I fear, and I am on your side.

15. Therefore, O Lord, will the blind and faithless be con-fronted with defeat, for they have no authority to challenge your ways.

16. It is your ways O God that are always righteous and always unquestionable.

17. Who is he that challenges you and defies you? If he does not understand, then let him be silent and let him pray for understanding.

18. Otherwise O Lord, he will be confounded and ashamed before his peers, for they will remember has brash and irresponsible words.

19. Even his words spoken in his authoritative and convincing voice; but it is your word that prevails in your time.

20. So let him that refutes you foolishly be silenced, ashamed and confounded; let him understand that your ways are higher than his ways.

21. As for me, I will submit to the voice of Jehovah God. I will willingly respond to your call: for you are my God and I am subject only to you.

22. However turbulent and tumultuous the storm may be, I will hold on to your promises.

23. For the promises of Jehovah are sure and stead-fast, and surely they shall all be delivered.

24. Amen and Amen.

Kingdom Psalm 44

The strength of the wicked is temporal, and his prosperity short lived.

My Lord, how the wicked thrive in their wickedness and prosper in their deceitful and delusive ways.

3. The wicked man enjoins himself to societies that have secret and unscrupulous agendas.

2. They organize them-selves as legal entities and they prey on the unwary and unsuspecting citizenry, even on the righteous.

4. They fraternize behind closed doors as they plot violence and devise fraudulent schemes to rob the poor and defraud the rich.

5. They all band them selves together with cords of sworn pledges and unethical codes of dishonor.

6. Their god is their greed and their commitment to their rituals, their tradition and their dark secrets.

7. Their oaths bind them to their own ungodly precepts and alienate them from the holy oracles of Jehovah; but Jehovah is the righteous God.

8. They are very powerful and influential in the scope of their dealings; for even governments they defraud and manipulate.

9. Their conspiracies run deep in the strata of society, and they thrive financially from their violence and their corruption.

10. O God, deliver the poor from the clutches of these oppressive extortionists and enrich their treasuries.

11. Exalt the humble in their very sight and establish them in authoritative positions.

12. Strengthen the hands of the weak on whom they prey and defend their integrity.

Kingdom Psalm 45

The church has lost its way and lost sight of its mission.

Have mercy on the church of God; for many are backslidden.

2. Many have fallen and become victims of tradition and legalism; they have succumbed to their own doctrines.

3. They seek approval from the status quo; they look to man for their glory and for acceptance.

4. They are flamboyant in their worship and theatrical in their praise; some worship their apparel more than they worship you.

5. They are snared in the thicket of ritualism and the atrics, and they compete for earthly glory.

6. Therefore, they have lost sight of their mission and their purpose to evangelize and save souls for the kingdom of God.

7. They have lost sight of dying men, broken homes and troubled nations; for the solutions lie within the God of the church.

8. For there is no power except Christ is head and there is no church except Christ is author and finisher thereof.

9. The church has encamped itself round about with cold lifeless walls of alienation.

10. Somehow, the church has separated itself from the multitudes of lost, hungry and dying souls that crave for a savior and a deliverer.

11. They have established a barrier between them and those that helplessly seek the bread of life and the way of life; they grope blindly in dark-ness.

12. cluttered the pathway with But the shepherds have conflict and confusion, and made the gospel conditional and inaccessible. You sent
13. So even the church itself dies because of the lack of knowledge because the lively knowledge of God's word is not diligently sought.

14. Also because the powerful enlightenment of your Holy Spirit is rejected and not pursued.

15. Heresies have crept into the pulpits; for even the abominable sins are openly manifested in the lives of the shepherds; the sheep are being deceived thereby.

16. They have proudly adorned themselves with crowns of abomination.

17. Even the plumes of wicked smoke rise from the kindled flames that burn from the altars.

18. They walk the road of death and are unaware because they are deceived by their own folly, for their end is disastrous.

19. I declare that the church has one fundamental doctrine on which it is built.

20. That is that Jesus Christ is the Son of the living God; he has been crucified, he arose and ascended into heaven.

21. He is King of Kings, Lord of Lords and savior of the world; his blood alone can wash you clean, for he is the long awaited Messiah.

Kingdom Psalm 46

Let your praise overcome your spirit and rejoice under the anointing.

I got a burning desire in my heart to praise the name of the living God, for he is majestic and royal.

2. My spirit is rejoicing in Jesus Christ and dancing in his glory; because he is the mighty God and glorious is his presence.

3. I will lift up my prayerful voice in a hallelujah praise and raise my holy hands in a joyous waive of jubilation.

4. I can feel the celestial glory coming down like holy acid rain; enough glory to bring dry bones to life and to make corpses to arise with a glorious hallelujah shout.

5. Oh that we would praise our majestic Lord with a tumultuous roar and shout a triumphant sound of praise right now.

6. Let's give glory to his holy name; let us magnify him with exuberance and dance joyfully in his holy presence in sanctified spiritual drunkenness.

7. Waive a right hand banner of thanksgiving until the anointing rattle your bones and ignite a fire in your loins.

8. Praise the Lord I say, praise the Lord; glorify him on the job; shout to him in the automobile on the highway.

9. Let his anointing fill your spirit and bring tremors to your body, hallelujah, hallelujah, hallelujah.

10. Even the highest praise is too low for Jehovah; for he is worthy, he is worthy! He is worthy!

11. Let the redeemed praise without shame and worship without fear.

12. Praise him and magnify him until your soul burst in flames of glorious anointing; until you are totally consumed by his Holy Spirit.

13. Praise him until you tremble and you can't contain yourself any longer; until 19. your shout is clearly heard by your neighbor and the dread of God comes upon him.

14. Glorify him until your co-worker is drunken by the overflow and electrified by 20. the excess glory.

15. Get up out of your seat and praise the Lord. Just feel his electrifying anointing; just let it flow and let it bless you with a shower of heavenly glory.

16. Oh it is so marvelous and magnificent when you praise him until your eyes are full and the tears begin to flow.

17. Just let them flow, for they are anointed tears of unspeakable joy and they are saturated with glory.

18. It is the supernatural presence of the Lord that you feel while in his presence. He is your God and your father; just magnify him and enjoy the ecstasy of his divine love and heavenly glory.

19. Oh how good and how joyous it is to be overwhelmed by the awesome presence of God and the infilling of his Holy Spirit. Hallelujah! Hallelujah Lord.

20. Great God of Zion, you are so marvelously wonderful, so glorious and so fulfilling. Hallelujah to the Lamb of God.

21. God I love you so much; your anointing is like a holy, raging wildfire shut up in the marrow of my shaking bones. Hallelujah. Sholaba!

22. It's you God that are truly sweeter than the honey-comb and more intoxicating than whisky; there really and truly is none like you Jehovah.

Kingdom Psalm 47

The time to give praises to Jehovah God is always.

Always is the time for praise and the season for thanksgiving, for God's ways are magnanimous and his multitude of blessings numberless.

2. Therefore, we aught not to limit the praise we give to him or schedule the time of our thanksgiving for him.

3. Always is the time for praise; so let praise continuously pour out of our mouths from the very depths of our hearts and the illuminated chasms of our spirit.

4. No matter how numerous our praises are, they can never compensate for the countless blessings already bestowed on us or those blessings yet to come.

5. The blessings of God flow by the moment and fall by the second, for we cannot live a millisecond without them.

6. Therefore, we aught to always be mindful of his goodness and appreciate him with our always praise.

7. For his divine worthiness far surpass our frail ability to applaud and to honor him.

8. Even the very breath that we breathe is a blessing from God and an element of his grace.

9. Therefore, we aught to praise God always because always is the time to praise him.

10. Let all the saints say Amen.

Kingdom Psalm 48

Christ is the unshakeable and unmovable foundation of the church of God.

Jesus Christ is my rock and my fortress; he is my solid foundation, and all other foundation is as quicksand.

2. He is the foundation of the church of God; indeed, he is firm and unshakeable.

3. Even the host of hell and the prince of darkness, who is its demonic god, can-not move its foundations.

4. Because it is steadfast and is as steady and everlasting footings.

5. It cannot be shifted or removed; for God is the architect, engineer and builder; and there is neither any error nor are there any flaws whatsoever.

6. The standard is perfection and is guaranteed forever and forever; it is flawless throughout all eternity.

7. Therefore, I am unmoved by the shifting winds of doctrine, the tidal waves of tribulation, or the buffeting about by trials and afflictions.

8. For Jesus Christ the divine foundation is able to withstand every adversarial force that comes against me; in fact, he has already done so on the cross; for he conquered them all.

9. Therefore I will stand even in the face of my enemy and even on the threshold of death; for Christ is my refuge and my deliverer.

10. He is my army and his favor is my weaponry; for my battles are his by inheritance; for I have exchanged them for victory and abundant life.

11. I am an over comer by heritage and made more than a conqueror by salvation through Jesus Christ.

12. Therefore when the storms of adversity rage on, I have no reason to tremble, for I shall not be shaken; I shall definitely not be moved, for my position in Christ is stabilized.

13. For it is immovably firm and secure.

14. Neither shall discouragement overtake me nor shall fear derail my holy pilgrimage, for I am totally unperturbed and my walk is steady and focused.

15. Because I am sure-footed in my daily Christian walk, and I am anchored in Christ and grounded in his eternal redemption.

Kingdom Psalm 49

Jehovah is too mighty and too merciful for mankind not to praise him.

What a mighty and awesome God we serve; he's invisible, yet he sees and he knows every thing.

2. His knowledge sur-passes that of man by far; indeed, he knew everything even before he formed the earth.

3. Moreover, he is able to do all things; for he alone is able to perform the impossible as a routine act.

4. Though he is not seen in action, he controls even the patterns of nature, for day and night are in his hand.

5. It is he who propels the earth on its axis and guides it through the universe, for he is its very architect and creator.

6. His power and his might are matchless and beyond the comprehension of men, for we have neither seen nor do we know the extent of his powers.

7. One exception is we know that they are without limitations and they are with-out restrictions; for he is Jehovah and there is no God like Jehovah.

8. He is yet a mystery even to men whom he created and gave dominion over all his earthly creations.

9. Because of his divinity, his ways are unfathomable even to mankind; except he reveals his mysteries they remain sealed and hidden.

10. Therefore brethren, he who challenges Jehovah is a fool, and he who defies him is worse than an infidel.

11. For God is supernatural and superior in all his being and miraculous and almighty in his prowess; he is not human that man should defy him.

12. Be it known also that he is not a man that man should be compared to him; he is the God who created man.

13. It is Jehovah who has given time its constraints and the universe its boundaries, for he is the God that created them both.

14. Even the sun and moon move to his will and obey his commands; for he is Lord even over the sun and the moon; they too are his creations.

15. He has given the oceans their depths and the mountains their heights; for they too he created.

16. For even the winds are stayed by his mighty hand and they puff with his breath. They respond to his com-mand, for it is Jehovah who is their source of origin and strength.

17. So who is man that he reviles God, and who are the children of men that they defy God?

18. They are but a miniscule particle of dust in his sight; yet he reveres them and deemed them worthy of honor and power.

19. Yet he esteems man and deems him worthy of his fellowship; yet he establishes a respectful and prized relationship with man.

20. How awesome is this God that he is so thoughtful of man and so loving toward him; even in the midst of man's rebellion and disobedience.

21. God cares for him even while man rejects him and denies him, and even while man forsakes his statutes.

22. Oh how mighty and forgiving is Jehovah God; and how merciful are his ways.

23. For we breathe his breath and yet we revile him with it; indeed we praise and honor his enemies with the breath he breathed into us.

24. How ungrateful and foolish is man? And how unthankful is he, for I have to conclude that he is suicidal in his ways, because the wages of sin is death.

25. Yet God is forgiving and merciful; yet he protects us and directs our paths; yet he restrains the murderous hand of Satan that is continuously against us.

26. O Let man denounce his foolish ways and praise the mighty Jehovah God; for he is alive and he has given us life; moreover, Jehovah reigns supreme. Hallelujah!

27. It is he that keeps us alive and also our children; even in the face of unseen danger he protects and delivers us all.

28. Let us all give him praises and thanksgiving; let us honor him as the Almighty God of the universe.

29. For he is too mighty and much too graceful to oppose; his love is too great toward us for us to be so rebellious and unthankful.

30. Forgive their foolish ways O Lord; remove the dark veil from their blinded eyes and let sinful men see you for who you really are before their sin permanently snare them.

31. My God, I recognize you as almighty and eternal; I praise you, I honor you and I magnify your royal and holy name. Sholaba!

Kingdom Psalm 50

The sure and deserving lot of the wicked is death and destruction.

O wicked and lawless men, whose sin has duped you into a false sense of security:

2. Be aware that there is one that is more exalted than you are, and one that is mightier than you as well.

3. Beware of your pride, for you are living on borrowed time.

4. The clock is not the master of time, but only its slave, for while it measures time, God is the provider thereof.

5. Seek God and surely you will find wisdom; then will your dark understanding be opened; then will you realize your limitations.

6. For you unknowingly depend on the same God who 13. you have rejected and denied; he is your very sustainer and provider.

7. Your pride is false; it is the result of your ignorance and the fact that you have denied the higher powers.

8. You are puffed up in self-righteousness because you have made yourself god, and you deny the divine deity of the infallible God.

9. Your recompense is hell; it is the wage for your chosen vocation in which you have arduously labored; for you have chosen it out of your own free will.

10. In humility of spirit and godly wisdom, I entreat you to forsake your haughtiness and reject your self-righteousness.

11. For they are a millstone around you neck and a snare to your feet.

12. They blur your vision and cloud your thoughts so that they are polluted and convoluted.

13. Therefore you cannot see your creator and you can-not hear the voice of your sustainer.

14. For he is mightier than you; he has created you and provides for you even now while you are in your foolish state of denial.

15. Free yourself from the bondage of ignorance and from the clutches of the evil one, for he is deceptive and misleading.

16. You were created to fellowship with the almighty creator and to abide in his presence.

17. Your heritage is much richer than the one you pursue, and more abundant in prosperity than the one you have chosen.

18. Let the Son shine into your heart and illuminate your spirit so that your eyes may be opened.

19. Welcome the Christ into your life so that your dark understanding may be enlightened.

20. Even now he knocks at the door of your heart and tugs at the imaginations of your mind, for he is anxious to deliver you.

21. Respond while he still allots you time and while he still affords you opportunity.

22. For one day he will still the hands of time and time will be no more, and the door will be closed to you.

23. I entreat you in the name of Jesus Christ that you answer the call of God as he invites you to an abundant and eternal life.

24. The end of your present path is terrible, and destruction is your sure and deserving lot.

25. For those are the deadly wages for which you so diligently and arduously labor.

Kingdom Psalm 51

May the saints of God be always honest in their dealings and not be self serving sometimes.

O Lord your sheep knows your voice, and yet they sometimes follow a stranger; for they hear you conveniently because their hearing is sometimes blatantly selective.

2. When they are hell bent on following their own chosen path, they are unable to hear your voice even though it is clear and succinct.

3. I marvel at their spirit of selfishness and greed and the convenient ease with which they put their righteousness on hold.

4. Even in the presence of the righteous, who is aware, they strive to impress the ungodly and defy your instruction.

5. Behold they are gullible and self-serving in their arrogant attitude; they clearly show that they do not fully trust in you.

6. They dare to expedite and accelerate their own agendas with total disregard for your timing and your directives.

7. They are impatient and will not wait on you; they refuse to allow you to carry out your plans unobstructed and unhindered.

8. However, you are not God just sometimes, but you are God always, when you please them and when you displease them.

9. In repetition, they rehearse this acknowledgement with their lips; even from the pulpit, it is their prophecy and their praise.

10. Yet their hearts fail them when they themselves are put to the test, and they renege on you.

11. Who is sincere in their hearing and trustworthy in their dealings? For Jehovah God requires genuine worshippers who are faithful and steadfast in their ways.

12. So let the saints of God display honesty and godliness at all times and in all seasons.

Biography: Honorable Oswald O'Neal Skippings

Born on the capital island of Grand Turk in 1953, Honorable Oswald Skippings has an illustrious political career that spans over thirty years. In 1976, he evolved from a tumultuous socio political environment from a frontline activist into a politician, who most people now refer to today as the most prolific and outstanding politician in the Turks and Caicos Islands. Incidentally, he is currently the longest serving politician in the Legislative Council of the country, having served for a period of 29 consecutive years of stalwart, unbroken service. Interestingly, the margin of his victory at the polls has progressively increased in the last two elections.

At a very early age, he assumed a cabinet position in the first ministerial government of the late great Hon. JAGS McCartney, first Chief Minister and national hero. Honorable Oswald Skippings served as Deputy Chief Minister, Minister of Health, Education, and Welfare and Local Government as a young man of 23 years old. He later served as Chief Minister some three years later after the untimely death of JAGS McCartney. He is still to date the youngest member to have served in the Legislative Council and the youngest to become Chief Minister in the Turks and Caicos Islands. Although not returned at the polls in 1980, he retained the leadership of the Peoples Democratic Movement, thereby becoming the second leader of the first political party. During this time, he piloted his party through many social and constitutional changes that were taking place within the islands. In 1988, he led his party to the greatest victory in the Turks and Caicos Islands' political history, His party, the Peoples

Democratic Movement, was returned with eleven (11) seats, leaving the Peoples National Party with two (2) seats. He became Chief Minister for the second time and assumed portfolio responsibility for tourism, communications, and transportation.

In 1995 and 1999, after his party won the general elections, his portfolio was increased and comprised of tourism, communications, transportation, immigration, labor and culture. At the helm of a ministry so vital to the economic viability and future of these islands, Hon. Skippings engineered an aggressive, yet tempered tourism growth, one of the fastest growing tourism industries in the region. The policies he initiated stimulated major private sector growth and a sound infrastructural base, while at the same time safeguarding the integrity of the islands' pristine environment and preserving their considerable natural assets. In his position as minister, he realized a tourism increase of over 800%, including significant increases in visitor repeat business. Under his watch, there were also major development projects to sustain such rapid growth including new hotels and resorts and the renovation and construction of the new airports in Providenciales and Grand Turk. This unprecedented growth in the tourism sector in particular has resulted in the unprecedented vibrancy of the islands' economy to the extent of some 13% plus economic growth in one year, allowing the Turks and Caicos Islands to be dubbed the star of the region by the Caribbean Development Bank. What was even a more spectacular feat was his ability to successfully negotiate agreements with a large number of commercial airlines to provide jet services to the islands from a number of international destinations.

Other projects include the enhancement and creation of new tourism products such as Little Water Cay Iguana Nature Park, thus contributing greatly to increased natural resource conservation. His testimony may be summed up in this visionary quote: "As tourism in the Turks and Caicos Islands grows rapidly in this new millennium, an important goal will be to stimulate economic well being and to develop new job opportunities, which will enhance and challenge the capabilities of the people of the Turks and Caicos Islands for years to come." At the same time, Hon Oswald O'Neal Skippings was mindful of the fragility of this industry and cautioned, "It is our duty to be the guardians of our rich heritage and our abundance of natural beauty, which is second to none." He was one of a few Caribbean leaders to have been honored with an award by the Caribbean Tourism Organization, in New York, for outstanding contribution to the development and promotion of tourism in the region.

Hon. Skippings was cognizant even then of the vital link between reliable, cutting edge communications and high-end, world-class tourism. He has over the years, through skillful and tenacious negotiations, ensured that digital communications, internet access and cellular services were launched in all the islands, and that the service was maintained at international standards. After over one hundred years of a monopoly situation, he also began the process for the liberalization of the telecommunication industry to ensure that these islands received the best and most affordable service available. During this communications revolution, he also saw to it that internet services were provided free of charge to all government schools.

In spite of the magnitude of his huge contribution to these islands and its economy through tourism, Hon Skippings is even better known for his great oratory skills, which catapult him in the upper echelons of the list of public speakers. He is well respected throughout these islands, regionally, and internationally for this God given talent.

Prior to his political career, Hon. Skippings spent a couple of years as a pupil teacher before attending Mico Teachers College in Jamaica. He prematurely terminated his course of study and answered the clarion call of his people to enter politics and provide them with quality representation in the legislature.

In May of 1984 after a soul stirring experience one night at home alone, he voluntarily surrendered his life to Christ the very next morning at his sister's dining room table. He later learned that she was at that time leading a group in prayer for his salvation. He is convinced that the success that he has experienced in his extensive political life and the progress and economic achievements that his country has experienced during his tenure in office are all because of the supernatural blessings of God. He sees the Turks and Caicos Islands as the "Israel of the Gentiles" and foresees it playing a major spiritual role in the future. He is also convinced that the fact that he is alive and has survived so long as a political leader, and was able to overcome all the snares and hurdles that have been placed in his path, is solely because of the unmerited grace of the Almighty God. He knows with assurance that his political career is ordained and called of God.

Hon. Skippings has in recent years recommitted his life to God and is now an avid Bible student. He preaches and teaches on occasion, and conducts Bible study once or twice weekly at Her Majesty's Prison on the island of Grand Turk. About fourteen years ago he did a ministerial internship program with the Church of God in Cleveland USA. He has his own ministry called Zion Praise, and recently came under the covering of Revival Faith Centre Ministry out of Fort Lauderdale, Florida.

Hon. Skippings is a father of five-four boys and one girl. He continues to live in the beautiful island of Grand Turk in the Turks and Caicos Islands. He is a gospel recording artists and a songwriter who has written scores of songs. He continues to enjoy his favorite hobby of writing and reciting his poetry and is also in the process of publishing his first book of poetry. He has a passion for the wholesome development of the youth.

The preservation, rejuvenation and development of culture is also one of his commitments. His life is a life of sterling service, and he is truly one of our greatest sons of the soil of the Turks and Caicos Islands.